Your Right To Know

How to Use The Law to Get Government Secrets

Jim Bronskill and David McKie

Self-Counsel Press
(a division of)
International Self-Counsel Press Ltd.
USA   Canada

DISCARDED

SQUAMISH PUBLIC LIBRARY

Copyright © 2014 by International Self-Counsel Press Ltd.

All rights reserved.

No part of this book may be reproduced or transmitted in any form by any means — graphic, electronic, or mechanical — without permission in writing from the publisher, except by a reviewer who may quote brief passages in a review.

Self-Counsel Press acknowledges the financial support of the Government of Canada through the Canada Book Fund (CBF) for our publishing activities.

Printed in Canada.

First edition: 2014

Library and Archives Canada Cataloguing in Publication

Bronskill, Jim, 1964-, author
   Your right to know : how to use the law to get government secrets / Jim Bronskill and David McKie.

(Legal series)
Issued in print and electronic formats.
ISBN 978-1-77040-211-9 (pbk.).—ISBN 978-1-77040-974-3 (epub).—
ISBN 978-1-77040-975-0 (kindle)

   1. Freedom of information—Canada. 2. Public records—Access control—Canada. I. McKie, David, 1959-, author II. Title. III. Series: Self-Counsel legal series

KE5325.B764 2014   342.71'0662   C2014-905617-6
KF5753 B764 2014

Foreword by Suzanne Legault, Information Commissioner of Canada, used with permission.

Self-Counsel Press
(a division of)
International Self-Counsel Press Ltd.

Bellingham, WA   North Vancouver, BC
        USA   Canada

Contents

Tables

Samples

Notice to Readers

Laws are constantly changing. Every effort is made to keep this publication as current as possible. However, the authors, the publisher, and the vendor of this book make no representations or warranties regarding the outcome or the use to which the information in this book is put and are not assuming any liability for any claims, losses, or damages arising out of the use of this book. The reader should not rely on the authors or the publisher of this book for any professional advice. Please be sure that you have the most recent edition.

Acknowledgements

The encouragement, inspiration and toil of many people have helped make this book possible. I want to thank the mentors who introduced me to freedom of information, namely Kirk LaPointe, editor-in-chief of Self-Counsel Press, who impressed the importance of using this tool upon a young journalist finding his way. Others from whom I have learned much about this subject over the years are Amir Attaran, Dean Beeby, Murray Brewster, Paul Champ, Rob Cribb, Michel Drapeau, Darrell Evans, Darce Fardy, Mike Gordon, Steve Hewitt, Dean Jobb, Mike Larsen, Jeff Lee, Andrew Mitrovica, Laura Neuman, David Pugliese, Ann Rees, Tom Riley, Alasdair Roberts, Ken Rubin, Fred Vallance-Jones, Kevin Walby, Wesley Wark, Reg Whitaker, and my co-author and teaching partner David McKie, whose admirable dedication to our craft is heartening. Thanks also go to the many professionals working in the access field who have diligently processed my requests and complaints, as well as the Canadian Association of Journalists, the Canadian Historical Association, The Canadian Press, and the Carleton School of Journalism and Communication. Finally, a special note of gratitude to Lucianne and Adam for their unending patience and support.

— JB

Given that Jim Bronksill and I have used our research methods course at Carleton University to teach students the ins and outs of using access-to-information and freedom-of-information laws, my primary acknowledgement must go to him. I've learned from Jim's attention to detail, his rigour and his professionalism; qualities that grace this book. Jim's acknowledgement list is a fine one, as I, too, have used many of those individuals as sources of information and inspiration. In addition, I would like to thank Carleton University's School of Journalism and Communication, which has given us the opportunity to hone our use and knowledge of the law that forms the heart of this book. More journalism schools must teach their students how to use these laws, which are fundamental for holding governments to account. To that end, it's essential that citizens shoulder the challenge. An individual who has been instrumental in including citizens in the conversation about our access laws is the commissioner, Suzanne Legault, whose foreword introduces this book. I have had the honour of being part of the Right to Know sessions her office holds in September. And, finally, my ultimate thanks go to my wife, Deirdre, our son, Jordan, and our daughters, Leila and Hannah Rose, and our son-in-law, Scott. They are the daily source of my inspiration and strength.

— DM

Foreword

I am often asked to explain why access to information is important to Canadians. In response, I point out that federal policies, programs, and laws touch so many aspects of our everyday lives — the regulation of health products, international travel, mail delivery, transportation, and food safety, just to name a few.

Canadians give their government the authority to spend their taxpayers' dollars, make policy decisions, and administer programs on their behalf. In return, they want to be informed of the rationale and outcome of government decisions and actions, they want to validate information that is provided to them, or they simply want to obtain more details about an issue of interest. Being able to request and receive government information empowers Canadians to participate in their democratic system.

In Canada, we are fortunate that access to government information has been embedded in most federal, provincial, and territorial laws for more than 30 years. It is true that the federal access legislation and its administration have not kept pace with the rapid proliferation and sophistication of information technologies and new business models being used today, but its purpose and goals still remain sound.

Given the limitations we are currently facing with the federal regime, now more than ever citizens should not take their right to know for granted. It is the role and the responsibility of all of us to champion the cause of transparency, to ensure accountability wherever taxpayers' dollars are being spent, and to nurture a culture of openness in Canada.

Although more and more Canadians are making access requests, for many, making a request may seem like an overwhelming task. That is why this guide is a fundamental tool, because it will help new users navigate the world of access to information and give them the confidence to exercise their right.

I congratulate Jim Bronskill and David McKie for taking on the task of writing *Your Right to Know: How to Use the Law to Get Government Secrets*.

This book will serve as a valuable resource for Canadians as they exercise their right to know.

Suzanne Legault
Information Commissioner of Canada, July 2014

Introduction

As journalists, we use freedom-of-information laws to help keep an eye on government institutions and other public bodies that do everything from police environmental regulations to protect people from terrorists. It has always been an important part of our jobs, and it has become increasingly necessary in an era of tightly scripted political messaging and rigorous information control.

But journalists are only proxies for the average citizen: We ask the questions and seek out the records you might if you had the time to explore issues of public importance. That's why we believe everyone with an interest in civic affairs can and should learn to use freedom-of-information laws to better inform themselves — and their communities — about the public agencies that touch so many aspects of our lives.

This guide is for the person who wants to know more about the safety of the air they breathe and the water they drink; the researcher curious about government grants to corporations; and the family that wants to discover what their grandfather did as a soldier during the war.

Our goal is to demystify the freedom-of-information process. Each year we ask the journalism students we teach whether they have ever filed an information request. Only a few put up their hands. And that's where we will begin, with an assumption you know little or nothing about using the laws. You might even have a bit of trepidation about making a request. Laws, after all, can be intimidating. Filling out a form can be tedious and confusing. Government agencies have become synonymous with red tape and bafflegab. And who has the time and money to do all this?

This guide will help you cut through the fog, with simple, step-by-step instructions on researching your subject of interest, drafting a request, dealing with agencies, and ultimately obtaining the records you seek — information that belongs to you.

Part One:
Background

1
History

Freedom of information can be traced to the Age of Enlightenment and Sweden's passage in 1766 of the first law to enshrine the principle of a public right of access to government records.

The King's ordinance,[1] issued in Stockholm, decreed that "loyal subjects may possess and make use of a complete and unrestricted freedom to make generally public in print" almost all government documents.

The driving force behind the law, Anders Chydenius,[2] was a priest and philosopher from rural Finland, which was then part of Sweden. His thinking had a profound and lasting effect on democratic development in the Nordic countries and the principles would later take root around the world.

Though it would be another 200 years before the United States passed its landmark *Freedom of Information Act*, the right to seek, receive, and impart information would be recognized in the Universal Declaration of Human Rights,[3] a 1948 resolution of the United Nations.

The right to information has since been reinforced as a tenet of international law through subsequent pronouncements and court rulings.

---

1 "The World's First Freedom of Information Act," Right to Information, accessed September, 2014. http://rtieng.wordpress.com/2011/07/29/the-worlds-first-freedom-of-information-act/
2 "Publication on the World's First Freedom of Information Act," Chydenius.net, accessed September, 2014. www.chydenius.net/eng/articles/artikkeli.asp?id=1021&referer=1&pages=1
3 "The Universal Declaration of Human Rights," UN.org, accessed September, 2014. www.un.org/en/documents/udhr/

Canada was among the first countries to institute a freedom-of-information law. The *Access to Information Act*[4] was passed in 1982 and took effect on Canada Day the following year. All provinces and territories have followed suit with their own legislation.

At last count, 99 countries[5] — from Australia to Yemen — had adopted laws.

According to an analysis by the group Right2Info,[6] the right of access to official information is constitutionally protected in 59 countries.

Various international organizations have advanced the cause through the creation of model laws and the promotion of high standards of openness.

The trend is clear: The right to information is seen as a key element of the cherished right of free expression, a seemingly unstoppable movement that could help entrench democracy worldwide.

---

4 *Access to Information Act*, Government of Canada, accessed September, 2014. http://laws-lois.justice.gc.ca/eng/acts/A-1/
5 "Countries with Access Regimes," FreedomInfo.org, accessed September, 2014. http://freedominfo.org/documents/Countriesaccesslist.pdf
6 "Constitutional Protections of the Right to Information," Right2Info.org, accessed September, 2014. www.right2info.org/constitutional-protections

2
The Laws

Governments have developed laws to guarantee, or at least facilitate, greater access to information. The main thrust of this book is Canada's federal law (the *Access to Information Act*) but, in general — whether we're discussing other jurisdictions such as provinces and municipalities, or foreign jurisdictions such as Sweden, the United Kingdom or the United States — access to records is a legal right to be fought for, protected, and enhanced. We will also cover essential information about the US federal law (the *Freedom of Information Act*), which helped kickstart the modern era's global drive for government transparency.

Though they may differ in specifics, the access-to-information or freedom-of-information laws, as they're called in provincial, municipal, and many foreign jurisdictions, embody the same general principles. The following sectiona discuss some of them.

1. The Right to Information

Though far from absolute, these laws assume that members of the public, no matter what they do for a living, how much money they make, or whether they are citizens of that particular jurisdiction, have the right to information that has been collected using taxpayers' money.

2. Balancing the Right to Know with Certain Protections

Few would argue that citizens should have the unfettered right to all government information. As a result, access-to-information laws contain provisions that categorize records, giving institutions the legal right to invoke secrecy when deemed necessary. For instance, the most sensitive records — such as those involving national security — are usually withheld entirely or in part.

3. The Privacy Side

Access-to-information laws are usually only one-half of the equation; the other half is privacy. The very same citizens demanding information should also have a reasonable expectation that details about their personal lives — such as medical and income tax records — stay private. That being said, citizens can use the privacy provisions to gain access to government records of their own personal history. For instance, you might want to know how the federal department responsible for unemployment insurance handled your file, or why one of its investigators knocked on your door to find out if you were really looking for work.

4. Fees

Although freedom of information is seen as a government service and a right, you are usually required to pay a minimal fee for the initial query, and then a bit more for any extensive searching that might have to be done. Such fees do not cover the actual cost of processing a request, nor are they meant to. Rather, they help defray a small percentage of government costs and remind requesters to be judicious in their use of the laws. Many argue there should be no fee for submitting an application.

4.1 Exemption from fees

Laws recognize that, in general, it is in the public good to release information. As such, some laws contain provisions that take public benefit into account, allowing for the fees to be waived. This could apply if the issue involved food or drug safety, for instance. Fee waivers will be discussed in Part Two: How to Request Information.

5. The Right to Complain

As the old rock 'n' roll refrain goes, "You can't always get what you want." The search fees may be too high, or the institution may have held back too much information, or taken too long to produce the records. In these instances, you have the right to complain to a commissioner or ombudsman who has legal powers to advocate on your behalf. We will look at the complaint process in Part Four: The Response to Your Request.

When used correctly, access laws can be powerful instruments of public policy and government accountability.

"The overarching purpose of access to information is to facilitate democracy. It does so in two related ways. It helps to ensure first, that citizens have the right to information required to participate meaningfully in the democratic process, and secondly, that politicians remain accountable in the citizenry."

— Supreme Court of Canada
in the 1997 case *Dagg v. Canada*
(Minister of Finance)

3
Who Uses Access to Information?

Because the Canadian federal access to information law gives citizens and others present in the country the right to request government records, no category of requester is supposed to get special favours; the law treats everyone equally. That being said, there are categories of requesters.

Treasury Board, the federal department responsible for administering the Act and collecting statistics, has created five broad categories: businesses, public, media, organizations, and academics.

Federal institutions covered by the law processed 55,145 requests for the fiscal year 2012–2013, a 28 percent increase over the previous year, and indicative of a trend that dates from 2006–2007.

As you can see in Table 1, members of the public comprised the greatest portion of the total number of requesters, a good indication that ordinary citizens are using a law designed to make government more accountable and accessible.

Traditionally, businesses have been the most prolific users, taking advantage of the Act to gather intelligence on competitors or simply to find out how their file is progressing through the regulatory process of departments such as Health, Transport, and Environment.

TABLE 1
ACCESS TO INFORMATION REQUESTS

Categories of requesters	2012–2013	Percent change from 2011–12 to 2012–13	2012–13 categories of the total number of requesters
Requests received from public	22,274	32%	40%
Requests received from businesses	21,242	14%	39%
Requests received from media	8,321	62%	15%
Requests received from organizations	2,415	24%	4%
Requests received from academics	893	56%	2%
Total	**55,145**	**28%**	**100%**

Source: Treasury Board/Info Source Bulletin
http://www.infosource.gc.ca/bulletin/2013/b/bulletin36b02-eng.asp

Though they are a growing segment of requesters, journalists have lagged behind — perhaps a sign of long-standing frustration with the obstacles to obtaining timely and newsworthy information.

Still, more Canadian journalists are turning to the Act to produce stories about such subjects as oil spills threatening the environment and Transport Canada's regulatory loopholes in the wake of the rail accident in Lac-Mégantic, Quebec, that claimed 47 lives.[1]

Organizations, a category that includes non-governmental organizations, lobby groups and politicians, represents individuals who have also become more frequent users, though still a small percentage of the total. Political parties file requests to obtain information, which they sometimes feed to reporters.

For instance, the Liberals requested information from the Privy Council Office (PCO), the link between the federal bureaucracy and the prime minister and his cabinet, for email correspondence dealing with the Senate scandal involving Mike Duffy and the Prime Minister's Office. When the PCO initially claimed there were no records, the Liberals went public with that claim, arguing that

---

1 "Death toll in Lac-Mégantic disaster now set at 47," CTVNews.ca, accessed September, 2014. www.ctvnews.ca/canada/death-toll-in-lac-megantic-disaster-now-set-at-47-1.1374099

the government seemed to have something to hide, and then filed a complaint[2] with the federal information commissioner.

Greenpeace has also been an active user of the law to uncover information about emissions from the oil and gas sector,[3] and the Alberta Federation of Labour has employed the law to gather statistics[4] on the federal government's controversial temporary foreign worker program.

The increased use notwithstanding, it's worth keeping in mind that the 55,145 requests filed in 2012–2013 represents a fraction of the number of annual applications the drafters of the Access to Information Act estimated would be filed when the law took effect on July 1, 1983.[5]

While the US government does not identify users by category to the same extent Canada does, there were 704,394 requests[6] in 2013 under the *Freedom of Information Act*. The departments of Homeland Security, Justice, and Defence topped the list of agencies receiving the most requests.

2 "Government withholding records on Senate scandal, Liberals allege," Canada.com,
   accessed September, 2014. www.canada.com/Government+withholding+records+Senate+scandal
   +Liberals+allege/9441404/story.html
3 "Memo contradicts Harper's stance on emission limits," TheGlobeandMail.com,
   accessed September, 2014. www.theglobeandmail.com/news/politics/memo-contradicts-harpers-
   stance-on-emission-limits/article18818653/#dashboard/follows
4 "Audit shows TFW program drives down wages, labour group says," CBC.ca,
   accessed September, 2014. www.cbc.ca/news/canada/edmonton/audit-shows-tfw-program-drives-
   down-wages-labour-group-says-1.2655129
5 Office of the Information Commissioner of Canada, accessed September, 2014.
   www.oic-ci.gc.ca/eng/lc-cj-abl-apl.aspx
6 FOIA.gov, accessed September, 2014. www.foia.gov

4
Getting Started

1. The Iceberg Theory

Icebergs may look huge, but you probably remember what your middle-school geography teacher said: Just 10 percent of this imposing wonder can be seen, with 90 percent hidden below the water.

It is much the same when it comes to government information. We can see a small portion of the material departments and agencies hold, while the rest remains tucked away — unless someone asks for it.

Agencies typically distribute news releases and informational bulletins, publish reports, and communicate through social media. Almost all of this material can be found through the institution's official website or Facebook and Twitter feeds. Generally, these are chances for the agency to present its activities in the best possible light. This makes perfect sense, as who would use their own website to post unflattering photos or notices about overdue bills?

Still, these highly visible sources of information are very helpful to the would-be requester. They provide a reliable and easily accessible means of finding out the agency's public stance or official line on the myriad issues for which it is responsible.

The news releases, backgrounders, and annual reports may answer many of your questions. But chances are they will leave some queries unanswered, or prompt new ones. And finding those answers will mean exploring the rest of the information iceberg.

There are two ways of doing so: informally, through web searches, phone calls and emails, and formally, by filing an access-to-Information request. Whether you end up making an application or not, it's a wise idea to start along the informal path.

2. Getting Started

Freedom-of-information laws are supposed to be a safety net, something one uses only as a last resort when other lines of inquiry fail.

In fact, the federal *Access to Information Act* says, "This Act is intended to complement and not replace existing procedures for access to government information and is not intended to limit in any way access to the type of government information that is normally available to the general public."

So, first you must ask, is it really necessary to file an access request?

It's a good idea to exhaust other avenues before taking the formal route. For instance, let's say your community group wants to know more about a coal-fired generating plant in your neighbourhood. You're aware that Environment Canada has done a report on the plant's emissions. Pick up the telephone or fire off an email to the department's general inquiries division to ask for a copy. This is often the quickest and easiest way to obtain government information. Increasingly, such simple requests are greeted with the response, "You have to go under Access to Information to get that." Remind the agency that the access law is intended to complement, not replace, an informal request. Make the representative tell you exactly why you must use the access law.

You might need to remind the official that, as a citizen, you have a right to know what your government and its agencies — in this case Environment Canada — are doing in your name.

Sometimes there are legitimate reasons why an agency might tell you to file an access request. Among the most common: The report contains personal, security-related, or commercially sensitive material than must be excised before release, or perhaps other departments that contributed to its creation must first be consulted.

Other kinds of records, including internal emails, briefing notes, and correspondence, often must also go through a similar review process.

However, in the interest of fuller disclosure, federal departments have begun proactively posting[1] various kinds of useful information, often under the heading Transparency: hospitality and travel expenses of politicians and public servants, contracts over $10,000, grant and contribution awards, position reclassifications, and cases of founded wrongdoing. Under the heading Publications, you will usually find an agency's annual report on plans and priorities[2] and performance reports,[3] which provide a wealth of details. Other material, such as audits and evaluations,[4] the annual public accounts,[5] and public opinion polls and focus-group reports[6], can be found on federal omnibus sites. Collectively these documents can paint a broad sketch of an agency, and may even provide some information on your topic of interest.

This is a good starting point, but it may be only the beginning of a long — and fruitful — journey.

3. Research

Before making the request, it's important to have a plan. As we've stressed, filing a request is a last resort when going the informal route — simply asking, for instance — fails to produce results.

One of the best tip sheets is the federal institution or department that regulates the activity you would like to investigate. Let's return to our example of the local coal-fired generating plant, which may be releasing too much carbon dioxide into the atmosphere. It's important to learn which departments are responsible for keeping an eye on the plant.

In this case the key department is Environment Canada. We learn from visiting the department's website that it is responsible for more than 80 regulations that govern certain activities of industries,

---

1   "Proactive Disclosure," Treasury Board of Canada Secretariat, accessed September, 2014. www.tbs-sct.gc.ca/pd-dp/index-eng.asp
2   "Reports on Plans and Priorities," Treasury Board of Canada Secretariat, accessed September, 2014. www.tbs-sct.gc.ca/rpp/index-eng.asp
3   "Departmental Performance Reports," Treasury Board of Canada Secretariat, accessed September, 2014. www.tbs-sct.gc.ca/dpr-rmr/index-eng.asp
4   "Audit and Evaluation Database," Treasury Board of Canada Secretariat, accessed September, 2014. www.tbs-sct.gc.ca/aedb-bdve/home-accueil-eng.aspx
5   "Public Accounts of Canada," Public Works and Government Services Canada, accessed September, 2014. www.tpsgc-pwgsc.gc.ca/recgen/cpc-pac/index-eng.html
6   "Public Opinion Research Reports," Government of Canada, accessed September, 2014. www.porr-rrop.gc.ca/index-e.html

other levels of government, trading partners, and Canadians in every region of the country.[7] *The Canadian Environmental Protection Act*[8] is responsible for dictating what chemicals can be released into the atmosphere and in what quantities. The Act stipulates a fixed amount the plant is allowed to emit, with the goal of phasing out these facilities and replacing them with plants that use a cleaner technology to produce energy.

It would also be helpful to find out what kinds of records Environment Canada produces by visiting a site called Info Source,[9] an online catalogue that provides a complete list of records listed by name, description, and category numbers the department uses to identify the information. Clicking on the List of Institutions[10] link provides a roster of about 250 institutions that are subject to the *Access to Information Act*, the *Privacy Act,* or both pieces of legislation, including rich background information about the agency and how it operates. Clicking on the Institutional Functions, Programs and Activities[11] link produces the inventory of records. For each record, there is a description, explanation of the types of records (e.g., correspondence, research studies, reports, meeting agendas, and minutes) and the record number. We'll learn more about Info Source in section 4. below, and in Chapters 5 and 15.

Now we know the Act that tells the plant how much it can legally pollute and we have a description of the records relating to the activity. Under the "Substance Management" section, we learn that the department is responsible for reducing the harm caused by toxic substances. As such, we may want to know what programs the department has put in place to entice, or indeed force, the plant to reduce its potentially harmful emissions.

The key is research: We must learn as much about the topic we're researching — and the agencies that might hold relevant records — before filing a request.

---

7 "Regulations," Environment Canada, accessed September, 2014.
   www.ec.gc.ca/default.asp?lang=En&n=4E972B4F-1
8 "Reduction of Carbon Dioxide Emissions from Coal-Fired Generation of Electricity Regulations
   (SOR/2012-167)," Environment Canada, accessed September, 2014. www.ec.gc.ca/lcpe-cepa/eng/
   regulations/detailReg.cfm?intReg=209
9 "Sources of Federal Government and Employee Information," InfoSource.gc.ca,
   accessed September, 2014. www.infosource.gc.ca/emp/emptb-eng.asp
10 "List of Institutions," InfoSource.gc.ca, accessed September, 2014.
   www.infosource.gc.ca/emp/emp05-eng.asp#chapters
11 "Institutional Functions, Programs and Activities," Environment Canada,
   accessed September, 2014. www.ec.gc.ca/default.asp?lang=En&n=F27D13FA-1&offset=2&toc=show

4. What You Know and What You Don't

By this point you should have a good sense of the tip of the iceberg — the publicly available information an agency holds on your topic of interest. In addition, through your research and a reading of Info Source, you should have a basic idea of the kinds of records you might want to request.

What exactly should you ask for? Before drafting an access-to-information application, it is a good idea to make two lists about the subject of interest: What you know and what you don't. This will help you pinpoint the gaps in your research and provide a basis for your formal request.

For instance, let's say you have found out which law is responsible for regulating the emissions from that coal-fired generating plant, and that Environment Canada is responsible for enforcing the law. You have also heard through the local grapevine that several senior federal managers have been briefed about the plant lately due to public concerns about its output, despite several queries — that a consultant hired by the department recently completed a report on the plant's emissions. You have asked informally for copies of the report, as well as any additional studies that may be available, but the department has declined to provide them to you.

That is what you know. Now for what you don't know:

- When was the latest emissions report and what were the results?

- What did officials say in their briefings? Was the minister briefed?

- Was a study undertaken and, if so, what does it say?

These are the outstanding questions that will form the basis of your Access to Information request.

Before we go any further, it's important to note that only Canadian citizens, permanent residents, and individuals or corporations present in Canada can use the federal *Access to Information Act*. It means citizens of other countries who do not live in Canada must find an agent eligible to make requests to do so on their behalf.

Part One Review

- Freedom of information is a public right with a centuries-long history.

- Laws in Canada and around the world embody many of the same key principles.

- The laws should be used as a last resort, not a first reflex.

- Thoroughly research your topic using open sources.

- Consult the federal Info Source guide or its equivalent in the relevant jurisdiction.

- Which institution(s) will have the information you seek? What is it you really want to know?

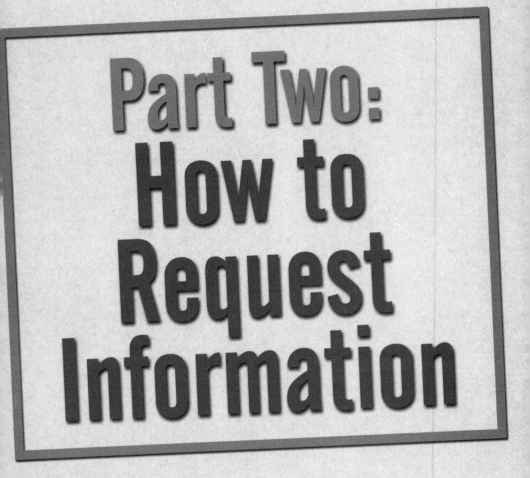

Part Two: How to Request Information

5
Writing a Request

You now know why you want to make a freedom-of-information request. To help prepare the application, you need to answer other basic questions: who, what, when, where, and how.

1. Who

In our example of the coal-fired generating plant, we've seen the importance of doing some basic research before drafting a request. Through a web search, we've discovered some valuable information on the Environment Canada website about the department's regulatory oversight of such generating plants. Using Info Source, we have also zeroed in on the types of records that might be of interest, as well as another helpful clue: other agencies where we could send requests.

Large departments like Environment Canada are surrounded by a constellation of related agencies that report to the minister of the lead department, carry out an arm's-length or quasi-judicial function, or serve as a watchdog. Sending requests to these agencies as well as the lead department can yield equally relevant records — documents that reflect the purpose and role of each agency. This can help reveal a fuller picture of the topic you're researching.

For instance, some sleuthing on the Environment Canada website and in the pages of Info Source tells us the Canadian Environmental Assessment Agency[1] — which works to minimize the

1 "About the Agency," Canadian Environmental Assessment Agency, accessed September, 2014. www.ceaa-acee.gc.ca/default.asp?lang=en&n=0046B0B2-1

impact of projects on the flora and fauna — has holdings that may be of interest. In addition, it says Environment Canada works with key federal partners: "The five natural resource departments — Agriculture and Agri-Food Canada, Fisheries and Oceans Canada, Health Canada, Natural Resources Canada, and Environment Canada — collaborate on research, share success stories, and disseminate information. This helps Canadians understand sustainable development issues and equips them to make and support informed decisions about sustainable development and the environment."

Using another example, perhaps you've heard the authorities are investigating environmental activists who regularly hold demonstrations outside the energy plant. You might ask Public Safety Canada for information, but in the course of your research you will note that the department oversees the Canadian Security Intelligence Service and the Royal Canadian Mounted Police, two satellite agencies that may also have records.

In the same vein, it is often worthwhile to send requests to various levels of government because in most cases public policy issues know few jurisdictional boundaries.

Be sure to pay careful attention to each access law you're using:

- Web links in Appendix II will help you get to know the laws governing various provinces, territories, municipalities, and public bodies.

- Fees, time limits, and other requirements vary depending on the jurisdiction.

- Be warned: Some jurisdictions levy large fees. A federal application costs $5 and those to British Columbia are free. However, a request under Alberta or Northwest Territories laws will cost $25.

- The biggest federal departments are often swamped with requests, so allow extra time when dealing with high-profile institutions.

- Applications to small agencies that receive few requests not only help round out your research, but often yield timely responses.

2. What

Public agencies generally use the catch-all term "records" for the various kinds of documents they hold, from old-fashioned memorandums to electronic messages. Though most records are textual in nature, they also include often overlooked ones (e.g., databases and audio and video recordings) we will explore Chapter 15.

Here are some of the most common kinds of records held by public agencies:

- Audits and evaluations: Internal examinations of programs to determine whether they meet agency objectives, provide value for money, and operate free of fraud and corruption. You'll find many of these records online. However, in other instances, you can obtain them only by filing a formal request.

- Public opinion polls: Survey results are also supposed to be posted online regularly, but not all turn up in a timely way, if at all.

- Reports and studies: References to the many reports that departments carry out or commission can often be found in lists of posted contracts, or in an agency's priorities and planning or performance reports.

- Briefing notes: Notes and memos are created on virtually all topics with which a department deals, often for the minister or deputy minister.

- Correspondence: Agencies still send old-fashioned letters, usually to outside recipients, as well as internal memos. However, email is much more common.

- Expense reports: Requesting copies of hospitality and travel expense claims, receipts, and invoices can provide much more detail than the summaries posted online.

- Routinely created documents: As you get to know a department, you will learn about the unique records it creates.

See Sample 1: Illustration of a briefing note intended for the Citizenship and Immigration minister to use in the House of Commons question period. Briefing notes are regularly prepared for federal cabinet ministers to help them answer questions during the daily question period.

SAMPLE 1
QUESTION PERIOD BRIEFING

Document Released Under the Access to Information Act / Document divulgué en vertu de la Loi sur l'accès à l'information.

QUESTION PERIOD NOTE

Date: January 18, 2007
Classification: unclassified
Agency: CIC

QP Note
Dual Citizenship

ISSUE: The evacuation of Canadian-Lebanese dual citizens has sparked a debate in the media on the issue of dual citizenship.

PROPOSED RESPONSE:

- We are not proposing legislative changes to dual citizenship. What we need to work out, as a society, are which rights and responsibilities of citizenship we want to emphasize.

- The recent Lebanese evacuation raised important issues such as ensuring more Canadians register with Canadian embassies and missions abroad. The Department of Foreign Affairs is leading a cross-government exercise to ensure these are addressed.

- The evacuation has also highlighted the need to ensure that all Canadians understand that they have rights and obligations as citizens.

- Canadians have expressed a diversity of views on dual citizenship which we will be studying carefully. They have told us that those who benefit from Canada's programs and services have a responsibility to contribute to Canadian society and the tax base.

- While my legislative priority with respect to citizenship is C-14, I would always be prepared, at the appropriate time, to look at other amendments to the Act.

CONTACT:	APPROVED BY:
Karen Mosher	Malcolm Brown
Director General, Citizenship	Assistant Deputy Minister, Strategic and Program Policy
Tel. No.: (613) 948-8600	Tel. No.: (613) 954-7353

1

000001

See also Sample 2: Illustration of an agency's uniquely created record.

After introducing Taser stun guns, the RCMP required officers to fill out a form each time they drew the powerful weapon from its holster. The forms included valuable information about how, when, and why officers used Tasers.

SAMPLE 2
UNIQUE AGENCY RECORD

CONDUCTED ENERGY WEAPON - ARME À PROPULSIONS

Weapon Type and Serial No. Type et no de série de l'arme P3-045660	Cartridge Serial No. No ce série des cartouches T03-022148	Fired Tirées ☐ Yes Oui ☑ No Non	Touch Stun Mode Mode paralysant ☑ Yes Oui ☐ No Non	Presence of Weapon known to Subject Présence de l'arme connue par le sujet ☑ Yes Oui ☐ No Non

CARTRIDGE #1 - CARTOUCHE #1

Distance from operator to subject (in metres) Distance de l'utilisateur au sujet (en mètres) .25	Spread distance between upper and lower probes (cm) Écart des sondes supérieure et inférieure (cm)	Duration of conducted energy (in seconds) Durée de l'énergie par conduction (en secondes)	Number of times fired Nombre de fois tirées

Verbal Command Given Ordre verbal donné ☑ Yes Oui ☐ No Non	Verbal Command Used - Ordre verbal utilisé Stop resisting or you will be hit with 50000 volts of electricity

Rationale for Using or Not Using Command - Motif d'utilisation ou de non-utilisation de l'ordre

attempt to de-esculate subject

Method of Sighting
Méthode de visée
None

Possible reason for any discrepancy - Raison possible de toute anomalie

☐ Moving Target
Cible mobile   ☐ Deflection (foreign object)
Déviation (objet étranger)   ☐ Operator Error
Erreur de l'utilisateur   ☐ Wind
Vent   ☐ Unknown
Inconnue   ☐ Other (Describe) ►
Autre (décrire)

Describe Clothing Barrier at **UPPER** and **LOWER** probes (composition, layers, thickness, penetration, etc.)
Décrire la barrière de vêtements aux sondes **SUPÉRIEURE** et **INFÉRIEURE** (composition, couches, épaisseur, pénétration, etc.)

Did probes penetrate subject's skin?
Les sondes ont-elles pénétré dans la peau du sujet?

Upper Probe - Sonde supérieure   Lower Probe - Sonde inférieure
☐ Yes Oui   ☐ No Non   ☐ Yes Oui   ☐ No Non

If yes, did probes remain embedded in subject's skin?
Dans l'affirmative, les sondes sont-elles restées enfoncées dans la peau du sujet?

Upper Probe - Sonde supérieure   Lower Probe - Sonde inférieure
☐ Yes Oui   ☐ No Non   ☐ Yes Oui   ☐ No Non

CARTRIDGE #1
CARTOUCHE #1

Point of Aim (upper probe only)
Point de visée (sonde supérieure seulement)

Point of Impact (upper probe)
Point d'impact (sonde supérieure)

Point of Impact (lower probe)
Point d'impact (sonde inférieure)

CARTRIDGE #2
CARTOUCHE #2

Point of Aim (upper probe only)
Point de visée (sonde supérieure seulement)

Point of Impact (upper probe)
Point d'impact (sonde supérieure)

Point of Impact (lower probe)
Point d'impact (sonde inférieure)

FRONT - DEVANT   BACK - DERRIÈRE

CARTRIDGE #2 - CARTOUCHE #2

Distance from operator to subject (in metres) Distance de l'utilisateur au sujet (en mètres)	Spread distance between upper and lower probes (cm) Écart des sondes supérieure et inférieure (cm)	Duration of conducted energy (in seconds) Durée de l'énergie par conduction (en secondes)	Number of times fired Nombre de fois tirées

Verbal Command Given Ordre verbal donné ☐ Yes Oui ☐ No Non	Verbal Command Used - Ordre verbal utilisé

RCMP GRC 3996 (2003-07) (FLC)   PAGE 2

3. When

Your request covers only records that already exist, meaning agencies are under no obligation to create documents or compile information for you (though some may be willing to do so in certain circumstances). Therefore, timing is important in two respects:

First, the time-frame covered by your request. For instance, you might ask for records created from July 1 to September 1, 2014. In general, asking for more than six months' worth of records can be troublesome.

Second, the point in time you submit the request. You must ask: Do the records I seek exist? If not, when are they likely to be created? If a political controversy erupts over your topic of interest, you might decide to wait a few days to capture any records created in the aftermath.

4. Where

Departments and agencies covered by access-to-information laws have dedicated units responsible for receiving, acknowledging, and processing your request. At a small federal agency, it might be a single person — known as a co-ordinator[2] — while at a large institution, there may be a dozen or more staff, known as analysts, who report to the co-ordinator.

Each agency devotes a portion of its website, usually in the Transparency section, to its Access to Information and Privacy functions. Here you will find contact information for submitting a request or making inquiries. Or you could consult the omnibus list of co-ordinators.

Provinces, territories, and many municipalities similarly publish information about their freedom-of-information laws on their websites, a list of which you will find in Appendix I.

A good place to begin learning about filing a federal request in the United States is the government *Freedom of Information Act*[3] portal at foia.gov.

The US National Freedom of Information Coalition[4] has compiled useful resources on filing requests at the federal and state

---

2 "Access to Information and Privacy Coordinators," Treasury Board of Canada Secretariat, accessed September, 2014.
   www.tbs-sct.gc.ca/atip-aiprp/apps/coords/index-eng.asp
3 FOIA.gov, accessed September, 2014. www.foia.gov/index.html
4 National Freedom of Information Coalition, accessed September, 2014. www.nfoic.org

levels at nfoic.org. The Reporters Committee for Freedom of the Press[5] has created a tool that allows users to create, file and track requests at the federal and state levels.

5. How

Most Canadian jurisdictions provide online access to a standard form[6] for making a request. The federal form is typical, asking the requester to state the agency to which you are inquiring, a brief description of the records sought and your contact information. It is a good idea to include your email address as many analysts prefer to deal with requesters this way, and it allows you to correspond with them at a time that suits your schedule.

The federal government has begun a pilot initiative[7] that allows requesters to apply to some — and likely eventually all — agencies online, paying the $5 fee electronically. However, at the time of this writing the more common (and cumbersome) method involves printing out a completed request form and mailing it with a $5 cheque. (If you prepare, say, three requests for the same agency, you can make the cheque for $15.) An additional note: Usually the cheque is made out to the Receiver General for Canada,[8] though some agencies require it to be made directly to them.

Fees, forms, and procedures vary between jurisdictions, so be sure to follow instructions carefully. For example, depending on the province, some municipal requests are made through the provincial law, while many large municipalities administer their own access programs. In the case of most municipal requests, there is no need to specify the department that might hold the records you seek. One exception is the police, who often accept requests directly. As a general rule, no matter the jurisdiction, you can dispense with the form and write a letter to the relevant agency, as long as you include the details needed for processing.

The US *Freedom of Information Act* has been on the books since 1966[9]. The states and the District of Columbia have similar laws, and the US *Privacy Act* was passed in 1974.

---

5   iFOIA.org, accessed September, 2014. www.ifoia.org/#!
6   "Access to Information Request Form," Treasury Board of Canada Secretariat, accessed September, 2014. www.tbs-sct.gc.ca/tbsf-fsct/350-57-eng.asp
7   Access to Information and Privacy (ATIP) Online Request, Government of Canada, accessed September, 2014. https://atip-aiprp.apps.gc.ca/atip/welcome.do?lang=en
8   "3.2.1 Departments in Alphabetic Order for 2013–2014," Public Works and Government Services Canada, accessed September, 2014. www.tpsgc-pwgsc.gc.ca/recgen/pceaf-gwcoa/1314/txt/rg-3-alpha-eng.html
9   "Federal Open Government Guide, 10th Edition," The Reporters Committee for Freedom of the Press, accessed September, 2014. http://rcfp.org/federal-open-government-guide

The US information law is wide-ranging,[10] covering agencies, departments, regulatory commissions, government-controlled corporations, and "other establishments" in the government's executive branch. Each federal institution subject to the law[11] has a designated FOIA Service Centre and a Chief FOIA Officer to manage the requests, which can be submitted in writing using forms, or simply by writing a letter. The actual wording of the request would follow the same lines that we've already discussed for filing requests in Canada.

As with the Canadian system, try the informal route before filing a formal request. See if the document or database is available online. Determine whether another requester such as a journalist or non-governmental organization (some environmental groups, for instance, have become aggressive users of the US FOIA) has already obtained the record. If the informal route fails, then try going formal by doing your homework (which includes determining the correct institution and finding its contact information) and then file a request.[12]

The US site for federal requests, foia.gov, includes intuitive links on where to direct your application.

There is no application fee for a US *Freedom of Information Act* request, which generally includes two hours of search time and 100 pages of photocopying.

It is common in the United States to state up front what you are willing to pay for the processing of your request. Regardless, if a federal agency believes it will cost more than $25, you will receive a written estimate of the fees.

The US law allows you to request a fee waiver, but you must persuade the agency that disclosure of the information sought is in the public interest and not primarily for commercial purposes.

It is therefore worthwhile to take the time to formulate tightly worded requests, with short time frames that stand a greater chance of success.

10 The Reporters Committee for Freedom of the Press, accessed September, 2014. https://www.documentcloud.org/documents/1212755-federal-open-government-guide-10th-edition-u-s.html#document/p7/a165166
11 "Federal Open Government Guide, 10th Edition," The Reporters Committee for Freedom of the Press, accessed September, 2014. https://www.documentcloud.org/documents/1212755-federal-open-government-guide-10th-edition-u-s.html#document/p9/a165167, accessed September, 2014.
12 "Federal Open Government Guide, 10th Edition," The Reporters Committee for Freedom of the Press, accessed September, 2014. https://www.documentcloud.org/documents/1212755-federal-open-government-guide-10th-edition-u-s.html#document/p33/a165171

Requesters can ask to have their application processed on an expedited basis if a delay would endanger someone's life or safety, or if the requester would suffer the loss of substantial due process rights.

It's also worth noting that you don't have to be an American citizen to file a request, a rule that similarly applies to other foreign jurisdictions, such as the United Kingdom and Mexico, that may be of interest to Canadian requesters.

Institutions have 20 working days to respond, though they can and do miss that deadline due to issues such as workload. So it's in your best interest to keep track of the request and contact the institution if it fails to respond within the promised time frame. If you are denied records because the agency has used the exemptions or excessive fees, you have the right to complain to the head of the institution.[13]

6. Drafting the Request

Returning to our example of the coal-fired generating plant, we might ask Environment Canada for: "Records — including but not limited to briefing notes circulated at the director general level or above, and all reports/studies — from July 1 through September 30, 2014, concerning carbon-dioxide emissions from the coal-fired generating plant in Saddleton, Alberta. Please do not process records that are obviously cabinet confidences. As this request is in the public interest, "I ask that all fees please be waived."

Note that we have:

- Indicated we want records, but also specified a few types using the phrase "including but not limited to."

- Kept the time frame tight (three months).

- Limited briefing notes to those circulated at a senior level.

- Specified we want only records related to carbon-dioxide emissions.

- Asked the analyst to put aside records that are likely confidences of the federal cabinet, as these fall outside the ambit of the law. More on this in a Chapter 11.

---

13 "Federal Open Government Guide, 10th Edition," The Reporters Committee for Freedom of the Press, accessed September, 2014. https://www.documentcloud.org/documents/1212755-federal-open-government-guide-10th-edition-u-s.html#document/p34/a165172, accessed September, 2014.

- Requested a fee waiver. While the federal law makes no specific reference to waiving fees above and beyond the $5 application amount, some jurisdictions do entertain such requests. It's a good idea in any event because, as we will see, fees are largely discretionary.

When drafting a request, pay particular attention to the time frame covered and the type of records you specify. This is where your research will pay dividends, allowing you to word the request accordingly. The key is striking a balance between wording that is too narrow and too broad. Asking for all records on the Saddleton generating plant for 2014 will prompt a message from an Environment Canada access analyst asking you to narrow your request. At the other end of the spectrum, it is best not to request specific documents, or records created on a particular day, unless you have solid research indicating this is likely to bear fruit.

In the case above, we might even break the request into two separate applications — one for briefing notes, the other for reports and studies.

If you're unsure of something about your request — wording, scope, type of record — you can call the access-to-information unit of the relevant agency to seek clarification. Under the federal law, these officials have a "duty to assist" you as a requester and should be able to answer basic questions. Some are more helpful than others, as service standards across government departments are rather uneven when it comes to freedom of information.

Create a separate file for each request. Make a copy of the request before sending it out and attach all subsequent correspondence with a paper clip. Even better, scan all pages and create a digital file for each request.

Emails can be voluminous, as most of us know from trying to manage our own inboxes. As a result, including emails in the scope of your request can cut into search time. If you really want emails, consider requesting them in a separate application. This is particularly helpful for high-profile topics, which tend to generate considerable internal email correspondence.

If you're interested in an agency's contracted studies but aren't quite sure of the subjects or titles, request a list or an inventory of the studies completed in the last year. Once you receive the list, you can make follow-up requests for the ones you want.

When requesting a document, such as a study, that you have read about in a newspaper article or government report, attach a copy of the reference to your request to help the analyst understand exactly what you're seeking.

If you cannot get a document one way, try a backdoor route. For example, the watchdog over the electronic spy agency Communications Security Establishment (CSEC) Canada is not covered by the access law. However, the watchdog's reports can be requested from CSEC, which does fall under the law.

Part Two Review

- Check relevant websites for forms, contacts, and information on departmental holdings.

- Questions? Call the access co-ordinator before making your request.

- When drafting your request, pay particular attention to the time frame and type of records.

- Make similar requests to more than one agency or government in Canada or the United States.

- Keep a photocopy or scan of each request and attach all return correspondence.

Part Three:
Follow-up

6
Acknowledgement Letter

Once you've thought about the record you want, crafted a request, and perhaps talked with the person handling your application to make the wording more precise, your work has only just begun. Now the process of obtaining records has entered a new phase, which begins with an acknowledgement letter. See Sample 3 for an illustration of a typical acknowledgement letter in Canada.

The acknowledgement is a letter from the department indicating the office has received your request. It should arrive within a week or 10 days after you send off a request. Some are pushing to have these transactions happen online, with acknowledgement in the form of an email. Indeed, some departments are moving in that direction.

However, for now, the old-fashioned method prevails. Under the department's logo, you'll notice the Access to Information unit's address. In the body of the letter, there is a reiteration of the wording, followed by a promise to process and provide the records as soon as possible, which means within the allotted 30 days or an extended period if necessary. In the event more than 30 days is required, a notice of an extension will be made in the acknowledgement letter or, more likely, in a second letter sent shortly afterward.

The letter usually closes with an invitation to contact the person assigned to your file should you have questions, and a reference to the all-important file number (A-2012-01772/CL3) in the top right-hand corner of the page. In most instances, there will be initials at the end of the number, separated by a forward slash or hyphen. These initials belong to the person or unit in the office handling the request. Departments use this file number to track your request. It is prudent to keep this letter handy, perhaps by scanning and storing it on your computer, or snapping a photo with your smart phone or mobile device and storing it on a hard drive.

Implicit in Canada's federal acknowledgement letter is payment of the $5 application fee. So the letter becomes a receipt for reimbursement if you're filing the request on behalf of an organization. Some agencies send a receipt as well, or you can request one.

Finally, the letter is signed by the department's Access to Information co-ordinator, who may process your request himself or herself — particularly if the agency is small — or, more likely, assign it to an analyst working in his or her unit. Either way, there should be sufficient information about who you can contact with any questions or concerns.

SAMPLE 3
ACKNOWLEDGEMENT LETTER

 Environment Environnement
Canada Canada
Terrasses de la Chaudière
10 Wellington Street, 4th Floor
Gatineau, Québec
K1A 0H3

Your File   Votre référence

Our File   Notre référence
A-2012-01772 / CL3

December 20, 2012

Mr. David McKie
CBC Radio Canada
181 Queen Street, 3rd Floor
Ottawa, Ontario K1P 1K9

Dear Mr. McKie,

This is to acknowledge receipt on December 20, 2012 of your request under the *Access to Information Act* for:

> **"I would like access to the list of briefing notes prepared for the minister from Sept. 1, 2012 to Dec. 11, 2012. Please exclude records deemed to be cabinet confidence or subject to third party review."**

We have started processing your request and will contact you as soon as possible. Please find enclosed our principles for assisting your request.

If you have any questions regarding this request, do not hesitate to contact me at 819-953-9750. Please quote the above file number on all future correspondence concerning this request.

Yours sincerely,

Colleen Leger
Access to Information and
Privacy Secretariat

Enclosure

7
Follow-up

1. Duty to Assist

The duty to assist is an important concept that should make it easier for you to get the information you want.

The measure, one of the few revisions to the *Access to Information Act* in more than three decades, took effect April 1, 2007. It affirms "a duty for institutions to assist requesters without regard for their identity."

This is more than a slogan; it's a responsibility that Access to Information co-ordinators should take seriously as a professional obligation to help make the government more accountable.

In its discussion1 of the importance of the duty to assist, the information commissioner concluded that it has two meanings:

1. It implies a commitment to a culture of service and underscores the importance of access to information as a service.

2. It changes the duty to assist from a moral obligation to a statutory one.

For the most part, Access to Information officials act with this obligation in mind. However, when negotiating for more records, lower fees, or quicker responses, friendly reminders about the need

---

1 "Chapter 6 — *Changes to the Access to Information Act*," Office of the Information Commissioner of Canada, accessed September, 2014. www.oic-ci.gc.ca/eng/rp-pr_ar-ra_2007-2008_10.aspx

to embrace that duty come in handy. The duty to assist also means helping you amend the wording or time frame of your request to ensure a solid chance of getting the records you seek. Remember, access-to-information officials may have a duty to assist, but you also have a duty to continue doing your homework during all stages of the process.

Principles for assisting applicants[2] published by the federal Treasury Board of Canada Secretariat:

In processing your request under the Act, we will:

1. *Process your request without regard to your identity.*

2. *Offer reasonable assistance throughout the request process.*

3. *Provide information on the Act, including information on the processing of your request and your right to complain to the Information Commissioner of Canada.*

4. *Inform you, as appropriate and without undue delay, when your request needs to be clarified.*

5. *Make every reasonable effort to locate and retrieve the requested records.*

6. *Apply limited and specific exemptions to the requested records.*

7. *Provide accurate and complete responses.*

8. *Provide timely access to the requested information.*

9. *Provide records in the format and official language requested, as appropriate.*

10. *Provide an appropriate location in the government institution where you can examine the requested information.*

Although a duty-to-assist provision may not be written into their laws, provincial and territorial freedom-of-information officials — and their ombudsmen — can be held, at least in spirit and practice, to the same standard.

US President Barack Obama has pledged to make his administration the most transparent in history. He and the attorney general have directed agencies to apply a presumption of openness

---

2 "Directive on the Administration of the *Access to Information Act*," Treasury Board of Canada Secretariat, accessed September, 2014. www.tbs-sct.gc.ca/pol/doc-eng.aspx?section=text&id=18310

when handling requests, which means invoking the spirit — not the letter — of the law in deciding whether to release information. This high-level directive is intended to foster a co-operative spirit between agencies and requesters. When departments fall short of these standards, it is worth reminding them of the president's words.

2. Follow-up

Depending on the complexity of your request, it may take more than one conversation or email exchange with the analyst handling it to set things straight.

An example: Say you're interested in flooding in your region, and you file an initial request with Aboriginal Affairs and Northern Development Canada for all records having to do with the damage caused by the river that flooded First Nations territory. It may turn out that the request is too broad, meaning the Access to Information unit's initial inquiries have identified thousands of pages of possibly relevant records in different branches of the department. The department may also have shared responsibility for the matter with agencies such as the National Defence, the Privy Council Office, and the province and municipality where the flooding has occurred.

This is where the continuing legwork comes into play. Never take for granted that the Access to Information official has all the answers or gives you the best advice right off the bat. It may be up to you to suggest limiting the request to records that originate within Aboriginal Affairs that do not require consultation with other agencies (a process known as third-party reviews). This could be a way of avoiding long delays and hefty fees. Perhaps it's also worth suggesting that the search be limited to the branch of Aboriginal Affairs responsible for working with First Nations to solve problems caused by floods.

You may be thinking that this legwork has already been done. But frequently, that is not the case. In fact, the follow-up continues as your request makes its way through the system. It's a good idea to check in regularly to see that things are moving along. Your request may become stalled. Staying in touch ensures that you can help the analyst remove any obstacles promptly.

In the freedom-of-information world, the squeaky wheel gets the grease. An access analyst might have 50 requests on his or her desk. But if you call or email regularly with polite inquiries about the progress of your request, it stands a much better chance of getting prompt attention.

If you're having trouble getting records from a public body and discover it is not subject to freedom of information, write the agency a letter seeking records as if it were bound by such a law. Explain that you believe the body has a duty to provide records in a timely way.

8
Keeping Track of Requests and Timing

1. Keeping Track

Now that you've sent the request and likely worked with the access-to-information office to smooth out the wording, it's time to make sure you document every step essential to keeping track of your request.

Keeping track depends on good organization. A first step might be setting up folders — whether hard copy or digital — to store your requests.

Once you've received the acknowledgement letter, create a folder for the correspondence and any follow-ups that contain re-jigged wording. It's also important to keep any articles of background information, or notes that you used in crafting the request. Use a paper clip to keep everything together.

If you have access to a digital scanner, scan the correspondence and articles (or save them as an electronic file if taken from an online site) and place them in a folder on your hard drive. Include the request number and a brief description in the file name so you can retrieve it easily.

Keeping track is also important because the access to information office will use the file number as a reference point when discussing the request.

Use a calendar to track when requests are due. Write the date on the acknowledgement letter or post it in an electronic file. If you have not received any acknowledgement on the due date, then the institution has made what's called a deemed refusal,[1] meaning it has failed to respond within the requisite time period.

The larger federal departments such as Environment, Health, and Transport should be sufficiently well-staffed to provide attentive service, but that can fall apart quickly[2] if the agency in question lacks enough analysts or suddenly finds itself burdened with a heavy workload. Smaller departments unaccustomed to handling many requests may also neglect to communicate with you. The same can be said for provincial and municipal institutions or those in the United States

Keeping track is essential, especially if you've made requests to several departments at the federal, provincial, and municipal levels. Otherwise, you will find yourself wondering whatever became of your requests, and scrambling to find bits and pieces of correspondence buried under the stacks of paper on your desk.

2. Extensions

Ideally, institutions would respond to access-to-information or freedom-of-information requests within the initial deadline — 30 days (including weekends and holidays) for federal requests.

However, this is usually a minimum, not a maximum.

There are two key reasons a federal agency may take additional time — known as an extension — to answer a request under the *Access to Information Act*:

- Section 9(1)(a), a request would interfere with operations of the institution. For instance, answering the request might involve an employee putting aside regular duties to search through a large number of records.

- Section 9(1)(b), the need to consult with third parties including other federal institutions, provincial and municipal governments, or individuals. The records may contain documents or other input from these parties, who have a say as to whether the information should be released.

---

1 "Info Source Bulletin Number 36B Statistical Reporting," InfoSource.gc.ca, accessed September, 2014. www.infosource.gc.ca/bulletin/2013/b/bulletin36b04-eng.asp#ftn3
2 "Length of Extensions Relating to *Access to Information Act* Requests," InfoSource.gc.ca, accessed September, 2014. www.infosource.gc.ca/bulletin/2013/b/bulletin36b02-eng.asp#ftnref3

According to the latest statistics, almost two-thirds of federal requests were answered within the 30-day time frame in 2012–13, an improvement over the previous year.

TABLE 2
FEDERAL ACCESS REQUESTS IN CANADA

Completion Time	Requests as Percentage		Number of Requests	
	2011–12	2012–13	2011–12	2012–13
0 to 30 days	55.3	64.8	24,128	34,997
31 to 60 days	21.3	17.3	9,313	9,331
61 to 120 days	12.9	9.8	5,639	5,294
121 to 180 days	3.9	3.4	1,712	1,847
181 to 365 days	3.6	2.8	1,575	1,542
More than 365 days	3	1.8	1,297	982
Total	**100**	**100**	**43,664**	**53,993**

Source: Info Source Bulletin Number 36B — Statistical Reporting

However, one-third of requests involved extensions ranging from 30 days to several months. When suspected confidences of cabinet — material that falls completely outside the access law — come within the scope of a request, it can take six months or more to process the application due to special procedures that must be followed.

Extensions are inevitable. However, the best way to ensure that you receive records within the initial 30-day period, or with as little delay as possible, is to craft well-researched and precisely worded requests.

"We are overloaded and we are short-staffed."

— Access to Information analyst
at a major federal department
explaining why a request was late,
August 2014

3. Delays

Delays are a frustrating part of the system — and impossible to avoid. So you'll need a good dose of patience and ingenuity. Extensions and fees are two of the main contributing factors to delays, according to investigations by the Treasury Board[3] and the information commissioner.[4]

Institutions use extensions to buy more time to consult with parties such as other departments, or to deal with large volumes of material. The Treasury Board report points out that institutions process ever larger amounts of material, especially email correspondence, which is becoming a standard communication tool for conducting government business. This reality, combined with an insufficient number of qualified access analysts, represents the "single largest reported cause of delays." In addition, tragic events such as the train derailment[5] in Quebec's Lac-Méntic in 2013, the 2008 listeriosis crisis, or hot political topics such as treatment of Afghan detainees, cause agencies to be inundated with requests. In the case of the train disaster, a beleaguered Transport Canada took extensions of 300 to 365 days.[6]

In handling a request for records about tainted meat, Health Canada might have to consult with the Canadian Food Inspection Agency or its federal counterpart in the United States. While the Food Inspection Agency is supposed to review the records and tell Health Canada to promptly indicate whether any exemptions might apply, the health regulator may miss the deadline or even drag its feet. In short, the agency being consulted can hold the primary department — and you the requester — hostage.

Delays can also be caused by cumbersome review and approval processes within agencies. An overflowing inbox or a lengthy vacation can leave records in limbo instead of on their way to you.

Agencies may also struggle to process large volumes because they have poor record-keeping practices or inadequate software. Admittedly, newer programs have made it easier for some of the

3 "Reducing Delays in the Processing of Access to Information Requests," Treasury Board of Canada Secretariat, accessed September, 2014. www.tbs-sct.gc.ca/atip-aiprp/tools/reduction/reductionpr-eng.asp?
4 "Out of Time: Special Report to Parliament 2008–2009 Systemic Issues Affecting Access to Information in Canada," Office of the Information Commissioner of Canada, accessed September, 2014. www.oic-ci.gc.ca/eng/rp-pr_spe-rep_rap-spe_rep-car_fic-ren_2008-2009.aspx
5 "Images and videos of the devastation of Lac-Méntic," TheGlobeandMail.com, accessed September, 2014. www.theglobeandmail.com/news/national/in-pakistans-capital-the-mega-mall-rises/article13050598/#dashboard/follows
6 Access to information: An essential tenet of democracy," Office of the Information Commissioner of Canada, accessed September, 2014. www.oic-ci.gc.ca/eng/rapport-annuel-annual-report_2013-2014_3.aspx

largest and busiest departments to deal with requests. However, many institutions are still burdened with outdated procedures, such as printing records and mailing them to other institutions, manually processing $5 application cheques (something that should change with the electronic-fee pilot project), and using regular postal mail to send requests.

It's no wonder that the Treasury Board and the information commissioner's office have been urging departments to modernize the way they handle requests. The move by governments at all levels to provide more information proactively through their open data[7] initiatives may provide a needed spark, but odds are the process will be slow, hampered by budget cuts and the struggle to recruit, train, and retain a healthy complement of access professionals.

For these reasons it's crucial to learn how to negotiate with agencies, which will help you navigate obstacles and speed up responses. (See Chapter 9 for more about negotiating.) It's also important to keep in touch with the analyst handling your file to see how things are going. Remember, the squeaky wheel gets the grease. This also helps avoid the surprise of a lengthy, unexpected delay that keeps you waiting for a response even after an extension has elapsed.

4. Fees

As a general rule, the only time you should have to open your wallet when making a federal request is to pay the initial $5 application fee.

If you've followed the advice in this book about keeping requests simple and time frames relatively short, additional costs should rarely come into play. The $5 covers five hours of search and preparation time, which should be sufficient to find the records you seek in the relevant branches of an agency.

However, if the request is so complicated or broadly worded that it ties up resources and interferes with the agency's regular tasks, then you have one of two options: Negotiate a simpler, less-ambitious request that significantly lowers or even eliminates the additional fees, or agree to pay them because the request is as precise as it can get.

---

7 Data.gc.ca, accessed September, 2014. http://data.gc.ca/eng?lang=En%252520

The same advice applies to provincial and municipal requests, though it has been the experience of this book's authors and many of their students that freedom-of-information applications at the lower levels of government run the risk of being more costly — partly because officials may not be as experienced at negotiating with requesters. As with most aspects of freedom of information, the tendency to levy fees will vary between jurisdictions, and even from one federal agency to another.

Federal institutions generally do not charge if the search takes them slightly past the initial five hours. Trouble begins when the search stretches into several hours, covering volumes of material from headquarters and the regions. In these cases, institutions charge $10 an hour. If there are extra levies, the rationale will be spelled out in a statement that may even include a breakdown of the hours and activities, as you can see in the startling example in Sample 4 in response to a request to Human Resources and Skills Development Canada regarding changes to unemployment insurance.

Sample 4
FEE STATEMENT

Human Resources and Skills Development Canada
Access to Information and Privacy
140 Promenade du Portage
Phase IV, Level 1, Mail stop 112
Gatineau, Québec K1A 0J9
Fax: 8199530659

FEE STATEMENT
A-2012-00107 / MG

To: Mr. David McKie
CBC News
181 Queen Street, 3rd Floor
Ottawa, Ontario
K1P 1K9

Date: June 28, 2012

Date	Description	Unit Cost	Quantity	Charge	Payment
2012-05-29	Application Fee		0.00	$5.00	
2012-06-01	Payment Received		0.00	$0.00	$5.00
2012-06-28	Searching	$10.00	1,999.00	$19,990.00	
2012-06-28	(Less 5 free hours)	$5.00	-10.00	$-50.00	
			Balance Owing:		$19,940.00

The key is not to panic, even when a department is demanding almost $20,000. You should never receive an invoice demanding payment unless you have clearly consented to the charges.

Sometimes an agency will request money to cover the cost of photocopies, though this is becoming less common as records are released in digital format. A handful of departments continue to disclose records in paper format, but charge photocopy fees only when the release is 100 pages or more. One way to avoid fees upon receiving such an estimate from a federal agency is to indicate you would like to examine copies in a government office by checking the relevant box on the Access to Information form or specifying that option in your letter. When the records are ready for release, the agency will call to set up a viewing appointment. While this is easier to do in Ottawa, where most access offices are located, arrangements can be made to view records in federal offices in other cities.

Consider a fee statement an invitation to negotiate, a tactic we will explore in Chapter. 9 In many instances, you'll be able to significantly reduce the dollar amount and save your money for making new requests.

The same is true for US federal requests. An agency that sends you a fee estimate should also offer the opportunity to rejig the scope of your request to avoid paying additional monies.

9
Negotiating

Even after your request is filed, the wording is not carved in stone. It can be changed to narrow or broaden the scope to better reflect the records you seek. In some cases, your request can be narrowed to avoid paying large fees, if you've received a fee statement.

When wording is too broad, the analyst handling the request may call or email you to suggest a more precise focus by limiting the time frame covered, the type of records, or both. At this point the analyst might have a sense — or even a precise list — of the sort of records that respond to your request. The analyst might tell you there are 300 pages of emails, 150 pages of briefing notes, and another 100 of internal reports. This exercise can be helpful because you're no longer doing a jigsaw puzzle entirely blindfolded; you can suddenly see the outline of various pieces and choose the ones that make the best fit.

The only possible drawback of a tweak to the wording of your request is that it often will restart the processing clock. Perhaps an agency has 30 days to respond to your request, and you negotiate new wording 8 or 10 days into the cycle. That means the clock is reset once you sign off on the revised wording. This is usually worth the delay, as it can pay off in the long run with a more focused request that yields worthwhile records.

Sometimes instead of an analyst's call suggesting a round of rewording, you will receive a letter outlining charges above and beyond the $5 application fee due to the additional time needed to search for and prepare the requested records. Federally, the rate is $2.50 for each additional 15 minutes ($10 an hour)[1] spent locating and retrieving records from the agency's files. For instance, cutting the period covered by your request to three months from six and eliminating emails from the scope might avoid the need for extra fees.

A series of correspondence (Samples 5 – 9) shows a request in progress.

Another tactic is to narrow your request by eliminating any records that require consultation with third parties, such as other government agencies or businesses. This can speed things along considerably given that such consultations can take several months to complete.

In many cases, you will want to keep these records within the ambit of your request, even if it means waiting out a lengthy consultation. However, there may well be records covered by your request that were created within the agency in question and therefore need no consultation with other departments or outside parties. You can request what is known as a partial release of these records while work continues on the remaining ones. Sometimes agencies are reluctant to do partial releases because it means more work for the analyst, or there may be little in the way of records that could be released at an early stage. Discussing options with the analyst should help you choose the best path.

As always, it's a good idea to record notes of any conversations or email exchanges with an analyst, including the date of the interaction, a brief summary, and any coming dates of note — for instance, plans for a partial release or a promise from the analyst to update you.

---

1 "Fees," Government of Canada, accessed September, 2014. http://laws-lois.justice.gc.ca/eng/regulations/sor-83-507/page-2.html#h-6

SAMPLE 5
REQUEST

Protected when completed

Government of Canada / Gouvernement du Canada

Info Source

Access to Information Request Form

For official use only

Note: Please refer to page 2 for further information.

Federal government institution Correctional Service of Canada

Provide details regarding the information being sought (e.g. subject matter, date range, type of records)

Reports, studies, memos and briefing notes from 2013 concerning the planned electronic monitoring pilot project. Please exclude emails without significant attachments. As this request is in the public interest, I ask that all fees please be waived. Please contact me when any records are ready for release.

Method of access preferred (Please choose one)
- [ ] Receive paper copies of the documents
- [X] Receive electronic copies of the documents
- [ ] Examine the documents in government offices

Name of applicant Jim Bronskill, The Canadian Press / jim.bronskill@thecanadianpress.com

Street, address, apartment 800-165 Sparks St.   **City or town** Ottawa

Province ON   **Postal Code** K1P 5B9   **Telephone number** 613-231-8653

This request for access to information under the *Access to Information Act* is being made by

- [X] a Canadian citizen, a permanent resident or an individual present in Canada, best described as: [X] media [ ] academia [ ] business [ ] organization [ ] member of the public [ ] decline to identify

OR [ ] a corporation present in Canada.

This information is collected for statistical purposes and is published annually on the Government of Canada *Info Source* website (www.infosource.gc.ca).

Please note that the institution may contact you to verify your identity and to confirm that you have a right of access under the *Access to Information Act*.   Jan. 3, 2014   **Date**

The personal information provided on this form is protected under the provisions of the *Access to Information Act* and the *Privacy Act* and is retained and used as described in Personal Information Bank PSU 901 of the institution to which this form is submitted.

TBC/CTC 350-0057E (Rev. 07/2014)

Canada

SAMPLE 6
INITIAL RESPONSE

Correctional Service   Service correctionnel
Canada   Canada

Access to Information & Privacy Division

340 Laurier Avenue West
Ottawa, Ontario
K1A 0P9

January 10, 2014

PROTECTED

Your file   Votre référence

Our file   Notre référence
A-2013-00482

Mr. Jim Bronskill
The Canadian Press
800-165 Sparks Street
Ottawa, Ontario K1P 5B9

Dear Mr. Bronskill:

This is to acknowledge receipt of your request pursuant to the *Access to Information Act*, which was received on January 10, 2014. Your request is for Reports, studies, memos and briefing notes from 2013 concerning the planned electronic monitoring pilot project. Please exclude emails without significant attachments.

Please find enclosed a receipt for the $5.00 application fee.

Should you have any questions, please do not hesitate to contact Ana Maria Blanchette at (613) 992-8322.

Sincerely,

Ana Blanchette

Marie-Josée Trudel
Deputy Director

Encl.

Canada

Correctional Service Canada   **Service correctionnel Canada**

Access to Information & Privacy Division

340 Laurier Avenue West
Ottawa, Ontario
K1A 0P9

January 13, 2014

Your file   Votre référence

Our file   Notre référence
A-2013-00482

Mr. Jim Bronskill
The Canadian Press
800-165 Sparks Street
Ottawa, Ontario K1P 5B9

Dear Mr. Bronskill:

This is further to your *Access to Information Act* request received on January 10, 2014 for: "reports, studies, memos and briefing notes from 2013 concerning the planned electronic monitoring pilot project. Please exclude emails without significant attachments."

Please be advised that an estimated fee has been assessed under subsection 11(2) of the Act for search and preparation. In order to process your request a deposit of 50%, $17.50 is required before the search and preparation is undertaken. Please note that the first 5 hours has been borne by our institution. It is important to note that this assessment does not include the cost of reproduction. These will be assessed at a later date and you will be notified. The attached Fee Notice provides an itemized account of the current charges. You may reduce the above fees by narrowing the scope of your request.

If you wish us to proceed with your request, please forward the required fees within 30 days of the date of this letter.   Your payment can be made by cheque or money order payable to the Receiver General of Canada and mailed to the address above. **Please note, if these fees are not received within 30 days of the date of this letter, we will consider your request abandoned and our file will be closed.**

You are entitled, within sixty days of the receipt of this notice, to register a complaint regarding the fees assessed. It should be forwarded to the Information Commissioner, Place de Ville, Tower B, 112 Kent Street, 7th Floor, Ottawa, Ontario, K1A 1H3.

Should you have any questions, please do not hesitate to contact Ana Maria Blanchette at (613) 992-8322.

Sincerely,

AM Blanchette

Marie-Josée Trudel
Deputy Director

Encl.

Canada

SAMPLE 8
FEE ESTIMATE

Estimate Invoice

Estimate Fee Invoice

13-01-2014 03:11:06 PM

Mr. Jim Bronskill
800-165 Sparks Street
Ottawa, Ontario
K1P 5B9
CANADA

Request Number:	A-2013-00482		**Invoice Number:**	INV-YYYY-00001
Request Date:	10-01-2014			
Source:	Media			

Item	Quantity	Units	Unit Price	Unit Total	
Application Fee	0			5	
Searching	3.50	per hr	10	35	
Sub-Total:					$40.00
Payment Received				($-5)	
Sub-Total:					($-5.00)
				Total:	$35.00
				Partial Payment Required:	$17.50

DETACH HERE

To ensure proper credit, please return this portion with your payment.

Request Number:	A-2013-00482
Invoice Number:	INV-YYYY-00001
Amount Due:	**$17.50**

Make check payable to: Receiver General

Mail to:
340 Laurier Avenue West
Ottawa Ontario K1A 0P9

Bronskill, Jim

From:	Blanchette Ana Maria (NHQ-AC) <AnaMaria.blanchette@csc-scc.gc.ca>
Sent:	Thursday, January 23, 2014 12:23 PM
To:	Bronskill, Jim
Subject:	RE: A-2013-00482

Hi Jim. I can confirm that these changes have been made and a new retrieval (call out) has been made. You request is no longer on hold.

Thanks.

From: Bronskill, Jim [mailto:Jim.Bronskill@thecanadianpress.com]
Sent: Thursday, January 23, 2014 11:57 AM
To: Blanchette Ana Maria (NHQ-AC)
Subject: RE: A-2013-00482

Hello Ana Maria,

As discussed, could you please modify the above-noted request to read:

"Reports, studies, memos and briefing notes from Aug. 1, 2013, to the present – circulated at the executive committee / ministerial level – concerning the planned electronic monitoring pilot project. Please exclude emails without significant attachments."

Please confirm that these changes will be made.

Thanks kindly,
Jim

From: Blanchette Ana Maria (NHQ-AC) [mailto:AnaMaria.blanchette@csc-scc.gc.ca]
Sent: Thursday, January 23, 2014 10:12 AM
To: Bronskill, Jim
Subject: A-2013-00482

Hi Jim,

As discussed.

Ana Maria Blanchette

Senior Analyst/Analyste principale

Correctional Service Canada/Service correctionnel du Canada

Telephone/Téléphone: 613-992-8322

1

Part Three Review

- Make sure you receive an acknowledgement letter for your request.

- Remember that the access analyst or co-ordinator has a duty to assist you, and it's important to follow up to keep the request on track.

- Extensions and fee estimates can lead to delays.

- Delays are inevitable but can be managed.

- Learning to negotiate with agencies can help remove obstacles to successfully completing your request.

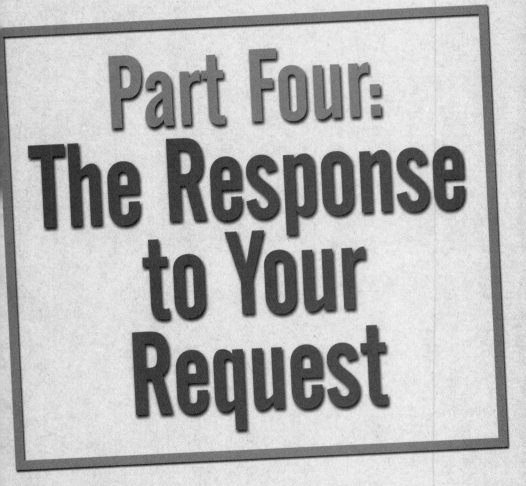

Part Four:
The Response
to Your
Request

10
Decoding the Information

It's the day you've been waiting for: It may take several months, but with any luck, one day you will open your mailbox to find a manila envelope from the agency that processed your request. Inside there may be just a few pages, a thick stack of paper, or a compact disc with a PDF file. Alternatively, agencies are increasingly willing to email PDF files as long as they are not too large to transmit easily.

Whatever the format or mode of delivery, there will also be a formal response letter from the agency informing you of the outcome of your application (see Sample 10). The letter might say:

- The records represent a partial release, with more likely to come.

- No records could be located.

- Some records are being released, but portions are withheld due to exemptions and/or exclusions (See Chapter 11).

- No records can be released due to complete exemptions and/ or exclusions.

Usually the letter will indicate that the file is now closed and that you have been provided with the records to which you are entitled. However, you still have work to do.

Deciphering access records is a little like reading tea leaves: They are often a jumble, presented in no particular order, and littered with strange acronyms and blacked-out (or whited-out) paragraphs, known as exemptions and sometimes referred to as redactions or severances. The pages may also lack titles, dates, and information about who created them.

For these reasons, when you receive documents it is important to return to your original notes and re-familiarize yourself with the issues. Then set aside some time to go through the documents carefully in a quiet space. If working with a hard copy, you might be tempted to reach for the yellow highlighter, but a better practice is to simply write notes in the margins. This will help in locating passages of interest once your review is complete. If the document is lengthy, you might make the notes on a separate sheet, recording the relevant page numbers.

For the more computer-savvy, a digital version can be uploaded to a cloud-based program such as DocumentCloud.org, which allows for easy highlighting, annotation, and sharing.

This is what we journalists like to call "interviewing the data," which means using the preparation and research that went into the request to ask informed questions about the material now sitting in front of you.

As you go through the records, look up unfamiliar words and names and include them in your notes, a practice known as "decoding" that can often be accomplished through quick online searches. When deciphering federal records, a visit to the government phone book called the Government Electronic Directory Services (GEDS) can reveal the names and titles of bureaucrats mentioned in briefing notes and emails. (See Sample 11 for how we decoded a series of Transport Canada emails.)

The one consistent concession to orderliness in a federal release package is the numbering of pages, usually in the bottom right-hand corner.

Given the scattered nature of the records, a chronology might help. Creating a time line of events based on the dates and times attached to the documents — especially emails — can make patterns emerge and assist you in determining what is truly new or interesting.

This is a particularly useful technique in documenting how a political drama unfolded or the way in which officials responded to a crisis.

Sometimes a phone call or email to the public affairs office of the department that released the records will be necessary to determine exactly what the documents are, including whether they are drafts or final versions.

The new elements, if any, should become clear after reviewing your original research, newly taken notes, and chronology. At the very least, you have a solid basis on which to quiz government officials and interested parties about the documents.

If you receive a hard-copy response to your request, scan or photocopy it to ensure you have a pristine copy for your records. This is also useful should you need to later share it with others.

How we decoded the information in the Transport Canada document (See Sample 11):

- tc.gc.ca = Transport Canada email address

- John Forster = Associate Assistant Deputy Minister Safety and Security, Transport Canada, Safety and Security Group, Tel. (613) 949-2394

- CIA = US Central Intelligence Agency

- CSIS = Canadian Security Intelligence Service

- GMT = Greenwich Mean Time (Time in Greenwich, England, which is the basis of standard time throughout the world.)

- CACO = Civil Aviation Contingency Operations

Managing and operating a 24-hour-a-day Aviation Operations Centre including an aviation reporting system involving the tracking of aviation-related incidents, accidents, and high-profile events for the purpose of keeping senior managers appraised of operations in the National Air Transportation System.

- Navcan = Nav Canada. Nav Canada co-ordinates the safe and efficient movement of aircraft in Canadian domestic air space and international air space assigned to Canadian control. Through its coast-to-coast operations, Nav Canada provides air traffic control, flight information, weather briefings, aeronautical information, airport advisory services, and electronic aids to navigation.

The quick decoding exercise above helped illuminate obscure elements of the emails about mysterious planes landing in Canada — aircraft that may have been connected to the US Central Intelligence Agency at a time when terrorism suspects were being ferried about the globe.

Transport   Transports
Canada   Canada

Access to Information and Privacy Division
Place de Ville, Tower C
Ottawa, Ontario
K1A 0N5

Your file   Votre référence

Facsimile: (613) 991-6594

Our file   Notre référence
A-2005-00726 / ay

MAR 1 5 2006

Mr. Jim Bronskill
The Canadian Press
165 Sparks Street
Suite 800
Ottawa, Ontario
K1P 5B9

Dear Mr. Bronskill:

This letter is in response to your request under the *Access to Information Act* for documentation pertaining to: **Aircraft allegedly controlled by the U.S. Central Intelligence Agency landing in Canada.**

I am pleased to provide the enclosed records (84 pages) that respond to this request. You will note that information is withheld from disclosure pursuant to 15(1)(d), 21(1)(a), 21(1)(b), 23 of the *Act*. (Copy of the relevant section(s) attached).

Should you have any questions, you may contact Ali Yassine at (613) 991-6583. You may file a complaint with the Information Commissioner at 112 Kent Street, 22nd Floor, Place de Ville, Tower B, Ottawa, Ontario, K1A 1H3.

Please quote the file number listed above in all correspondence pertaining to this request.

Yours sincerely,

Ginette Pilon
A/Coordinator
Enclosure(s):

Canada

03-0068 (93-10)

SAMPLE 11
EMAILS: DECODING THE INFORMATION

-----Original Message-----
From: Legault, Nicole <LEGAULN@tc.gc.ca>
To: Forster, John <FORSTEJ@tc.gc.ca>; LeCours, Jean <LECOURJ@tc.gc.ca>; Normoyle, Debra
<NORMOYD@tc.gc.ca>; Grégoire, Marc <GREGOIM@tc.gc.ca>; Vermette, Vanessa
<VERMETV@tc.gc.ca>
CC: TC Intelligence <TC-Intelligence@tc.gc.ca>; Lefebvre, Stéphane <LEFEBVS@tc.gc.ca>;
Ladouceur, Denis <LADOUDE@tc.gc.ca>
Sent: Sun Nov 20 14:13:26 2005
Subject: Re: Information concerning flight N196D

John,

I contacted CACO when I read your message at 2:00. Benoit Chagnon is dealing with another
priority (accident involving deaths) and said that he would assist as soon as he can.
Navcan is checking if billing information is available.

Nicole

-----Original Message-----
From: Forster, John <FORSTEJ@tc.gc.ca>
To: Legault, Nicole <LEGAULN@tc.gc.ca>; LeCours, Jean <LECOURJ@tc.gc.ca>; Normoyle, Debra
<NORMOYD@tc.gc.ca>; Grégoire, Marc <GREGOIM@tc.gc.ca>; Vermette, Vanessa
<VERMETV@tc.gc.ca>
CC: TC Intelligence <TCIntelligence@tc.gc.ca>; Lefebvre, Stéphane <LEFEBVS@tc.gc.ca>;
Ladouceur, Denis <LADOUDE@tc.gc.ca>
Sent: Sun Nov 20 13:35:47 2005
Subject: Re: Information concerning flight N196D

Nicole, thanks for this. Can you confirm owner of plane asap please.

-----Original Message-----
From: Legault, Nicole <LEGAULN@tc.gc.ca>
To: LeCours, Jean <LECOURJ@tc.gc.ca>; Normoyle, Debra <NORMOYD@tc.gc.ca>; Forster, John
<FORSTEJ@tc.gc.ca>; Grégoire, Marc <GREGOIM@tc.gc.ca>; Vermette, Vanessa
<VERMETV@tc.gc.ca>
CC: TC Intelligence <TCIntelligence@tc.gc.ca>; Lefebvre, Stéphane <LEFEBVS@tc.gc.ca>;
Ladouceur, Denis <LADOUDE@tc.gc.ca>
Sent: Sun Nov 20 12:55:14 2005
Subject: Information concerning flight N196D

Navcan confirms flight arrived in St John's Newfoundland on November 17, 2005 14:17GMT and
departed November 18, 2005 at 11:39GMT for Manchester. N196D is a twin turbo mini cargo
aircarft that can be fitted to carry 40 passengers.

Andre from Navcan will provide information on similar flights to St John's and their
frequency (as indicated in press) Monday morning. It is possible that aircraft was
accompanied by a Beach 200 aircraft. Will also confirm tomorrow.

                    15(1)d)

He said that someone from the media had called FAC saying there was a CIA plane in Canada.
Morin asked if we had heard about this. He had no other info.

Stephane said no and that pursuant to section 17 of the CSIS Act the CIA could be visiting
CSIS and suggested that Morin call CSIS to know if this was the case. Also, Stepahne
noted that if there was a plane illegally flying in Canadian airspace, we would have been
alerted by NACVAN, CACO or NDCC. He suggested he called NAVCAN to see of NAVCAN know about
such a plane.

Dan said he would call if he got more to ask or to follow up. Stepahne briefed the Duty
Officer (Jacques) in case there was a follow up to do. We did not hear back from them and
I could not reach them today.   000057

                                         2

11
Exemptions and Exclusions

1. Exemptions

"Ask and ye shall receive," the old saying goes. With freedom of information, a more accurate one would be, "Ask and you will get portions of some requested records."

The federal *Access to Information Act* contains several clauses[1] that allow agencies to withhold records from release for specific reasons. Provincial and territorial laws have similar exemptions.

The exemptions scheme may make freedom of information seem like a misnomer. How can information truly be considered free with so many exceptions and loopholes? However, few would argue that all government information should be disclosed. Doing so would make it difficult for officials to plan, deliberate, and decide everything from the need for a new stop sign at the corner to the wisdom of economic sanctions against a foreign power.

Some of the most common categories of information that qualify for exemption and the relevant section of the *Access to Information Act*:

- Personal information (about someone other than the requester)/Section 19.

- Details of international relations, defence, or national security/ Section 15(1).

---

1 "Archived — Access to Information Guidelines — Specific Exemptions," Treasury Board of Canada Secretariat, accessed September, 2014. www.tbs-sct.gc.ca/pol/doc-eng.aspx?section=text&id=13784

- Operations of government, including advice and recommendations from officials/Section 21(1).

- Information related to law enforcement or investigation/Sections 16(1)–(3), 16(3), 16.1(1) (a-d), 16.5.

- Third-party information, such as commercial confidences/Sections 20(1)(a–d).

- Legal advice and other material covered by solicitor–client privilege/Section 23.

Some are mandatory, meaning agencies must apply them, while others are discretionary. Exemptions may be applied to just a few words or entire documents. Several categories of exemptions might be sprinkled throughout a set of records. It can be difficult to determine which exemption applies to which passage because agencies are obliged only to list the exemptions applied to the records as a whole, not provide a line-by-line explanation.

Exemptions are supposed to be the judiciously applied exceptions, not the rule. And they should not be an excuse for agencies to shield embarrassing material from public view. If you suspect information has been improperly withheld, you can complain to an impartial ombudsman, an option we will discuss in Chapter 13.

As you can see from Table 3, the section of the act that protects personal information comprised almost 35 percent of the total number of exemptions for 2012–2013, the most recent statistics available.

The exemption ensures individuals dealing with a federal institution can expect that their identity will be keep confidential, with very limited exceptions. Provincial and municipal freedom-of-information laws also embrace the principle.

The use of national security-related exemptions under section 15 rose dramatically in the years following the 9/11 terrorist attacks on the United States.

Perhaps the most problematic of the most common exemptions is section 21, operations of government. This section has been the subject of many court cases and has been called the "Mack Truck" exemption,[2] meaning that it's so large authorities can invoke it to

---

2 "Murray Rankin on An Act to amend the *Access to Information Act* (transparency and duty to document)," OpenParliament.ca, accessed September, 2014. http://openparliament.ca/debates/2014/3/5/murray-rankin-1/only

withhold information that should be a matter of public record. Information used in the deliberations of cabinet ministers, their senior staff, and high-ranking federal bureaucrats accounted for almost 84 percent of all the exemptions in this category.

Section 16(1)–(4) is a very detailed set of provisions that cover instances in which records are produced in the course of investigations by police and officers of Parliament such as the chief electoral officer, information commissioner, and the auditor general. These records are withheld during investigations so as not to compromise the outcome.

Section 20 concerns information that so-called third parties — such as businesses regulated by departments like Health or Transport — submit to federal authorities.

Solicitor-client privilege enjoys a high level of protection in the Canadian legal system, meaning it can be difficult to challenge an exemption applied under Section 23.

TABLE 3
CANADIAN EXEMPTIONS 2012–2013

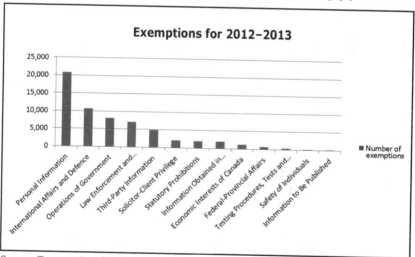

Source: Treasury Board/Info Source Bulletin
http://www.infosource.gc.ca/bulletin/2013/b/bulletin36b02-eng.asp

Trying to make sense of a document with exemptions can mean reading between the lines. But often there is enough in the release to provide genuine insight into how the agency is dealing with the topic of interest.

Be careful not to assume you know what's missing – the best you can do is an educated guess based on the clues and your knowledge of the file. This can be valuable fodder for follow-up questions.

See Sample 12 for an illustration of an exemption.

SAMPLE 12
EXEMPTION

Officials invoked Section 19(1) of the federal *Access to Information Act* to excise personal information from this RCMP document — the names of people who reported seeing a peculiar object in the sky above the Bedford Highway in Nova Scotia (Source: Library and Archives Canada).

2. Exclusions

If exemptions are discouraging, another category of denial — exclusions — can be downright depressing. The federal access law applies to material that may qualify for exemption and, when discretion applies, it can be released to the requester. Excluded records fall outside the law, meaning there is no discretion.

In these instances, Sections 68 and 69 of the Act[3] dictate that institutions are legally obliged to withhold the information in its entirety. Because the records are beyond the law's scope, even the information commissioner has no right to review them. In the event of a complaint from the requester, the commissioner is limited to pressing the government to re-examine the records and satisfy him or her that they are indeed confidences.

Section 68 covers three types of records: Published material members of the public can purchase; material used by libraries and museums; and material placed in the Library and Archives Canada, the National Gallery of Canada, or the various national museums "on behalf of persons or organizations other than government institutions."

Section 69, which frequently bedevils journalists, excludes records considered to be matters of cabinet confidence. In other words, records that the Prime Minister and his or her cabinet use to make decisions. Critics feel governments use this section to hide information that is merely embarrassing rather than truly confidential, which is one of the reasons successive information commissioners have pushed for the right to actually see the excluded records for themselves.

Liberal and Conservative governments have ignored the pleas. The result? When an institution relies on one of these sections to exclude information, the avenue of appeal is rather narrow. Still, it can be worthwhile to complain, as institutions have been known to mistakenly claim confidences.

---

3 "Exclusions," Government of Canada, accessed September, 2014.
  http://laws-lois.justice.gc.ca/eng/acts/A-1/page-27.html#h-29

There's a bit of good news: Cabinet discussion papers are accessible to requesters if the decisions to which the papers relate have been made public. For instance, if the government announces plans to buy new fighter jets, any cabinet discussion paper on that topic should be accessible under the access law. If the discussion paper relates to a cabinet decision that has not been made public, then the paper becomes accessible after four years. The difficulty there, of course, is knowing to ask for a paper about a secret government decision.

Finally, all cabinet confidences come under the law's purview after 20 years. While some argue the time period should be much shorter, minutes of cabinet meetings from two decades earlier can shine a light on relatively recent history.

In a similar vein, the US *Freedom of Information Act* has nine categories of exemptions under which information can be withheld. However, agencies can use discretion to release exempted information if there is no evident harm to governmental or private interests. In addition, the law includes three specific exemptions for certain information related to law enforcement or national security.

See Sample 13 for an illustration of a 1990 cabinet record in which the Progressive Conservative government of Brian Mulroney discusses the ill-fated Meech Lake constitutional accord.

SAMPLE 13
CABINET RECORD

Document Released Under the Access to Information Act / Document divulgué en vertu de la Loi sur l'accès à l'information.

SECRET — 10 —

CABINET DOCUMENT DU CABINET DOCUMENT DU CABINET DOCUMENT DU CABINET DOCUMENT

With respect to Quebec, the Prime Minister noted that Premier Wells had in effect done the work of Mr. Trudeau and Mr. Chrétien. He described Premier Wells as Mr. Trudeau's agent. Mr. Chrétien, hopeful of shortly gaining the Liberal leadership, had been silent. Premier Wells had enforced silence on the members of his own legislature. He had gagged them; nothing could be more serious. The Prime Minister contrasted this with the openness of his own Government's approach to capital punishment and abortion. The people of Quebec, he said, would see clearly that the work of Newfoundland was linked to the activities of Mr. Chrétien and that all of this in turn was linked back to the influence of Mr. Trudeau. Therefore, Premier Wells should be forced to face the only issue that mattered: he made a solemn undertaking, he had signed the document of June 9, he gave a commitment and had himself written in an endorsement undertaking to make every effort to achieve a decision and to be fully supportive if the Accord were passed.

The Prime Minister urged his colleagues not to be diverted by quibbles about who spoke to whom and when. The issue was simple. He had outlined it. He wanted all Ministers to have a copy of the agreement of June 9 so that as they left the Cabinet room that evening they would be in a position to explain clearly exactly how the situation had come about. How, he asked, can a provincial legislature approve an agreement made by the Premier if the Premier prevents the issue from coming to a vote. He said that at 7:30 p.m. that evening Senator Murray would speak to the press and he would have with him at that time the signed copy of the agreement. As for the Liberal Convention currently going on in Calgary, the Prime Minister noted that the Liberal party had participated in a colossal deceit and betrayal of the country. He said this was a critically historical moment. Premier Wells made an undertaking to vote and then he cancelled that vote.

The Prime Minister said that the quote in the Globe & Mail to the effect that he had waited until the last minute to "roll the dice" was false. He said the next accusation would be that Senator Murray deliberately did not return Premier Wells telephone call that morning so as to leave the Premier no time to reflect on how best to proceed before learning of the Government's proposal to make a reference to the Supreme Court provided Newfoundland supported the Accord.

[Ministers took a short recess in order to watch the proceedings in the Newfoundland legislature]

The Prime Minister said that it was now clear that the Accord was dead and that he would the next day give a speech that would make it clear that the country goes on and the Government is in control. He would not be aggressive nor would he be partisan; he would explain in detail exactly what had happened and how. He said that he would also speak to Quebecers on Sunday.

The Minister of Industry, Science and Technology, (Mr. B. Bouchard), speaking on behalf of his Quebec colleagues, said that it was a sad day.

s.14

He could not say what would happen next, but, he wished to pay tribute to the Prime Minister; he had worked closely with the Prime Minister

SECRET

000953

Source: Privy Council Office

12
Gaps in the Laws

In Canada, with the passage of the *Federal Accountability Act*, the federal government added agents of Parliament, federal Crown Corporations (including Canada Post and the CBC), and three foundations to the list of institutions covered by the *Access to Information Act*.

Still, some 100 entities with federal ties — including Nav Canada, the Canada Health Infoway, and large airport authorities — fall outside the law.

The government says it is still seeking advice on where to "draw the line" when it comes to placing more bodies under the Act.

For the time being some central institutions remain beyond the law's reach: the House of Commons, the Senate, the judiciary, and ministerial offices including the Prime Minister's Office.

Parliament has been under increased scrutiny[1] due to questionable spending by some senators, prompting renewed calls for expansion of the access law to cover the administrative activities of politicians. Any federally funded institution responsible for developing public policy in areas such as health, the environment, or transportation should not be able to escape the attention of the public.

---

1 "Spending scandal: Auditor general calls for independent review of MPs expense claims," TheStar.com, accessed September, 2014. www.thestar.com/news/canada/2013/11/19/spending_scandal_auditor_general_calls_for_independent_review_of_mps_expense_claims.html

Some suggest MPs and senators need a safe place — beyond parliamentary committees — to debate crucial policies in an unfettered manner without the fear of their discussions ending up in media reports. However, there would be little danger of that happening should Parliament be brought under the law. Confidential information, including dealings with constituents, would be subject to the protections discussed in Chapter 11, exemptions.

The Halifax-based Centre for Law and Democracy says Canada is lagging behind.[2]

"In countries around the world — including less established democracies than Canada such as India, Serbia, and South Africa — the law applies to all three branches of government, not only without any negative consequences, but with positive consequences."

2 Response to the OIC Call for Dialogue: Recommendations for Improving the Right to Information in Canada, Centre for Law and Democracy, accessed September, 2014. https://www.documentcloud.org/documents/1239933-canada-rti-jan13.html#document/p8/a169718

13
Complaints

1. Filing a Complaint in Canada

Institutions may have a right under the law to exempt or completely withhold records, but that same law gives you the right to complain to the Office of the Information Commissioner, an independent officer of Parliament who serves as a watchdog. You can also complain at the provincial or municipal level[1] to a commissioner or ombudsman.

The commissioner lacks order-making powers, instead relying on strong investigative powers and moral suasion to ensure the requester's rights are respected.

Some reasons to complain:

- An excessive time extension.

- Undue delays in processing a request.

- Large fees.

- Poor service that flouts the duty to assist.

- Exemptions or exclusions you feel have been unfairly applied.

The information commissioner has powers to review complete versions of records to gauge whether exemptions have been properly applied. As discussed in Chapter 11, the commissioner's ability

---

1 "Links," Office of the Information Commissioner of Canada, accessed September, 2014. www.oic-ci.gc.ca/eng/links-liens.aspx

to review excluded records is limited to obtaining a formal statement from the government that they are indeed confidences of the federal cabinet.

There are two ways to complain. The first is by filling out a form you can find on the section of the commissioner's website[2] that walks you through lodging a complaint. Sample 14 is the first page of the standard six-page form you can download and complete.

The remaining pages provide space to identify the institution that handled your request and indicate why you are dissatisfied.

You can also write a simple letter, as in Sample 15.

Be sure to include your contact information, the information commissioner's co-ordinates, the date, the name of the department that handled the request, the file number, and — in very plain language — your concerns.

Though not required, you can specify which sections of the Act you believe have been misapplied. As well, it is sometimes helpful to cite particular pages in the response package with objectionable exemptions.

It is also advisable to include copies of your original request and all correspondence from the department, including the acknowledgement and response letters.

The Sample 15 complaint is about a lengthy extension, one of the most common grievances the information commissioner's office handles, according to her most recent annual report.[3]

The complaint letter, or form, must be faxed to the number (identified on the form's first page, or the commissioner's website) or mailed within 60 days of receiving a response to the request in question. Once you've filed the complaint, you will receive an acknowledgement letter, similar to the one you got after filing the request. You can see acknowledgement of this complaint in Sample 16.

After the commissioner's office sends an acknowledgement letter and later assigns an investigator, the individual may contact you for further details. In some instances, the investigator may try to mediate a resolution, which means avoiding the far lengthier

2 "Lodging a Complaint," Office of the Information Commissioner of Canada, accessed September, 2014. www.oic-ci.gc.ca/eng/lc-cj-logde-complaint-deposer-plainte.aspx
3 "Annual Report 2013–2014," Information Commissioner of Canada, acccessed September, 2014. https://www.documentcloud.org/documents/1210785-2013-2014-annual-report.html#document/p15/a164745

SAMPLE 14
CANADIAN ACCESS TO INFORMATION COMPLAINT FORM

Commissariat
à l'information
du Canada

Office of the
Information Commissioner
of Canada

Access to Information Act
Complaint Form

The Office of the Information Commissioner of Canada (OIC) reviews the complaints of persons who believe that federal institutions have not respected their rights under the *Access to Information Act.*

If you wish to file a complaint with the Office of the Information Commissioner of Canada, please complete this form and send it with any accompanying documents, by mail or by fax to:

Office of the Information Commissioner of Canada
30 Victoria Street
Gatineau, Québec K1A 1H3

Fax: 819-994-1768

NOTE: At the present time, we do not accept complaints via electronic mail.

More information to assist you in completing this form is available at http://www.oic-ci.gc.ca/eng/lc-ci-logde-complaint-deposer-plainte.aspx or by calling toll-free in Canada 1-800-267-0441.

1) To expedite the processing of your complaint, please provide as much information as possible.

2) Complaints must be made to the OIC in writing within 60 days of receiving your response or a notice from the federal institution, or when you become aware that grounds for a complaint exist.

The personal information provided on this form is protected under the provisions of the *Access to Information Act* and the *Privacy Act*. Please note that your name and the details of your complaint will be provided to the institution that is the subject of the complaint.

*Required field

First name *		Last name *	
Mailing address *			
City *	**Province ***		**Postal code ***
Contact phone number*	**Alternative phone number**		**Fax number**
( )	( )		( )
Email address			
Please indicate the best time to contact you, as well as any contact restrictions:			
(The OIC's hours of business are Monday to Friday, 8:30 am – 5:00 pm EST)			

David McKie
181 Queen Street
Ottawa, Ontario
K1Y 1E4
288-6523 (office)
288-6490 (fax)
290-7380 (cell)
david_mckie@cbc.ca

The Information Commissioner of Canada
Place de Ville, Tower B
112 Kent Street, 7th Floor
Ottawa, Ontario
K1A 1H3
819-994-1768 (fax)
1-800-267-0441 (office)

general@infocom.gc.ca

March 30, 2014

Dear, Ms. Legault. I'm complaining about Natural Resources Canada's the extensions applied to my request for "Summer 2013 update on the fuel quality directive". The reasoning was spelled out in the May 22, 2014 response (DC7040-13-295). This follows a complaint after the department applied for a 300-day extension.

Please see the scanned letter below.

Thanks in advance for your cooperation.

Please acknowledge that you have received this letter and identify the investigator who will be handling the file.

David McKie

SAMPLE 16
COMPLAINT ACKNOWLEDGEMENT LETTER

Commissariat Office of the
à l'information Information Commissioner
du Canada of Canada

Gatineau, Canada
K1A 1H3

June 16, 2014

Mr. David McKie
CBC Radio News
181 Queen Street, 3rd Floor
Ottawa ON K1P 1K9

Subject: **Our file:** 3214-00408
Institution's file: DC 7040-13-295

Dear Mr. McKie:

This is to acknowledge receipt of your refusal complaint dated May 30, 2014, under the *Access to Information Act*, against Natural Resources Canada.

If you have any representations or additional information about your complaint, please do not hesitate to contact us. Also, if you are moving, please provide us with your new address and telephone number to ensure we can reach you once the file is assigned to an investigator.

You can rest assured that an official from our office will contact you as soon as possible.

Yours sincerely,

Carole Audette
Manager, Intake Unit

process of a formal investigation, which can take several months. Mediation seeks to find common ground between the requester and the institution, and can lead to the release of records in a fraction of the time it takes to complete a formal investigation.

Whether the matter is handled through mediation or investigation, the information commissioner will summarize his or her findings in a letter to you, including whether your complaint was well-founded. The determination is not necessarily the final word. If you feel strongly about pursuing an unsuccessful complaint, you can take the case to the Federal Court of Canada. In some cases, the information commissioner may ask the Federal Court to review a file when a resolution between requester and agency proves elusive.

An investigation can last several months, with exemption probes usually taking longer than those involving delays.

Due to the commissioner's intervention in the case shown in Samples 15 and 16, a lengthy delay was shortened.

The watchdog is also sometimes successful at persuading agencies to release more information, as in the case illustrated in Sample 17.

Sample 17: A page from a speech by a senior official of Communications Security Establishment Canada, the electronic spy agency. The first image is from an initial Access to Information release, while the second was disclosed after a successful appeal to the information commissioner.

2. Filing a Complaint in the United States

Though the process of lodging an official complaint is similar, there are some differences. It's worth taking a few moments to explain key steps in the process.

If you've been denied information, were asking to pay excessive fees, or suffered exceedingly long delays, there may be no choice but to appeal. The deadline for contesting a decision is 30 days — or in some cases 60 days — from the date the agency denied the request, withheld records, or demanded too much money or extra time. As in Canada, the US agency in question must explain that you have a right to appeal and provide contact information of the person or office within the agency that handles appeals. There may also be other instructions such as appeal deadlines. It is important to follow the instructions carefully to ensure that the appeal is accepted. If the agency fails to supply information about appeals, contact the agency's Freedom of Information Liaison Officer.

The process[4] is an administrative one in which you formally ask the agency to reconsider its position, which could result in the release of more records, the reduction or elimination of fees, or an acceleration of processing times for the records in question. Though the complaint is addressed to the agency's boss, it is really senior officials and attorneys who review the initial decision to determine if it should be upheld or reversed. The law gives the agency 20 days to make a decision.

The Reporters Committee for Freedom of the Press,[5] a non-profit association that gives journalists free legal advice, says the letter (and it should be a letter, instead of a form) must be "thorough and persuasive."[6] The committee also provides a template letter[7] that you can use as a guide. See Sample 18.

The committee advises you to make it clear you are submitting an appeal, and provide a summary of your request and the agency's response. You may also want to attach any other relevant correspondence with the agency. Also be sure to include all of your contact information at the top.

If the agency's final decision upholds the previous one, you have one of two choices: go to court, or contact an ombudsman called the Office of Government Information Services.[8] Though you are free to bypass the administrative process we've described and go directly to the office, it's advisable to do exactly as we've suggested.

---

4 "Federal FOIA Appeals Guide," Reporters Committee for Freedom of the Press, accessede October, 2014. http://www.rcfp.org/federal-foia-appeals-guide/administrative-appeals-process/what-can-i-appeal
5 "Federal Open Government Guide," Reporters Committee for Freedom of the Press, accessed September, 2014. www.rcfp.org/federal-open-government-guide
6 "What Should I Say in My Appeal Letter?" Reporters Committee for Freedom of the Press, accessed October, 2014. www.rcfp.org/federal-foia-appeals-guide/administrative-appeals-process/what-should-i-say-my-appeal-letter
7 "FOIA Letter Generator," Reporters Committee for Freedom of the Press, accessed September, 2014. http://rcfp.org/foia?op=show_form&type=fed_complaint
8 "The Office of Government Information Services," Office of Government Information Services (OGIS), accessed September, 2014. https://ogis.archives.gov/?p=//ogis/index.html

SAMPLE 17
TWO ILLUSTRATIONS:
BEFORE AND AFTER COMPLAINING)

RELEASED UNDER AIA INFORMATION UNCLASSIFIED

DIVULGUÉ EN VERTU DE LA LAI RENSEIGNEMENTS NON
CLASSIFIÉS

s.15(1)
s.19(1)

Speech by Shelly Bruce to IAFIE -- 26 May 2010

And what an eclectic program it is. The skills required are vast and sometimes rare: mathematicians, cryptanalysts, engineers, computer scientists, intelligence analysts and more.

While each discipline is fascinating in its own right, today we are here to talk about analysis in contemporary SIGINT. I'd like to tell you about how our SIGINT analysts spend their days, what this reveals about them and their job, and about the implications this has for their education. A lot of what we do is familiar -- it has deep historical roots and much in common with the other intelligence sub-disciplines. But much of it is specific to our mission, and to the technology, and it is this area where there may be opportunities and challenges for intelligence educators.

So I know an analyst named Justine. This is what she did yesterday, the 25th of May. She arrived at 7:30; we start early. She spent three hours reviewing data that had been compiled for her by software that had been working overnight; it's software that she partially wrote herself. She has constructed a hypothesis

. Unfortunately, the data will take a lot of tweaking before it's ready to support or reject the hypothesis.

She then attended an interview with a job candidate who has an
, but who is worried about working at CSEC because it might alienate her family and friends. Justine was there to evaluate her language abilities,

After a coffee break, Justine hopped in a cab and headed over to CSIS, where she met with a roomful of people from various departments to talk about how
There was much disagreement, because resources are tight. She had lunch at CSIS because their cafeteria is better than ours.

Back at CSEC, Justine returned to the data she'd been reviewing that morning. Her hypothesis seemed to be headed for the trash heap, but
which may be useful for the next investigation. Unfortunately, some of the data is garbled, but

3

A0313699-3-000003

SAMPLE 17 — CONTINUED

RELEASED UNDER THE AIA -- UNCLASSIFIED INFORMATION
DIVULGUÉ EN VERTU DE LA LAI -- RENSEIGNEMENTS NON CLASSIFIÉS

Speech by Shelly Bruce to IAFIE -- 26 May 2010

Last June, I returned to CSEC to head up the SIGINT program. And what an eclectic program it is. The skills required are vast and sometimes rare: mathematicians, cryptanalysts, engineers, computer scientists, intelligence analysts and more.

While each discipline is fascinating in its own right, today we are here to talk about analysis in contemporary SIGINT. I'd like to tell you about how our SIGINT analysts spend their days, what this reveals about them and their job, and about the implications this has for their education. A lot of what we do is familiar -- it has deep historical roots and much in common with the other intelligence sub-disciplines. But much of it is specific to our mission, and to the technology, and it is this area where there may be opportunities and challenges for intelligence educators.

So I know an analyst named Justine. This is what she did yesterday, the 25th of May. She arrived at 7:30; we start early. She spent three hours reviewing data that had been compiled for her by software that had been working overnight; it's software that she partially wrote herself. She has constructed a hypothesis about how her targets may be using certain communications technologies to further their cause. Unfortunately, the data will take a lot of tweaking before it's ready to support or reject the hypothesis.

She then attended an interview with a job candidate who has an important and rare target language, but who is worried about working at CSEC because it might alienate her family and friends. Justine was there to evaluate her language abilities, but quickly became a sounding board for the candidate's concerns because she's a member of the same ethnic community.

After a coffee break, Justine hopped in a cab and headed over to CSIS, where she met with a roomful of people from various departments to talk about how intelligence collection can be improved against a particular client set. There was much disagreement, because resources are tight. She had lunch at CSIS because their cafeteria is better than ours.

Back at CSEC, Justine returned to the data she'd been reviewing that morning. Her hypothesis seemed to be headed for the trash heap, but she's seeing some other patterns, this time linguistic, which may be useful for the next investigation. Unfortunately, some of the data is garbled, but

3

A0313699_3-000003

SAMPLE 18
US TEMPLATE LETTER

Your address
Daytime phone number

Date

Agency Administrator
Agency
Address

FOIA Appeal

Dear Admmistrator:

This is an appeal under the Freedom of Information Act, 5 U.S.C.§ 552.

On (date) I made a FOIA request to your agency for (brief description of what you request-ed). On (date), your agency denied my request on the grounds that (state the reasons given by the agency). Copies of my request and the denial are enclosed.

(When the agency delays:) It has been (state number) business days since my request was received by your agency. This period clearly exceeds the 20 days provided by the statute, thus I deem my request denied.A copy of my correspondence and the postal form showing receopt by your office are enclosed.

The information which I have requested is clearly releasable under FOIA and, in my opinion,may not validly be protected by any of the Act's exemptions.

(Here, insert legal and "public policy" arguments in favor of disclosure, if you wish. You are not required to make legal or poilcy arguments to support your appeal; if you simply state "I appeal" the agency will review the documents and the justifications given in the original denial. However, it is usually a good idea to try to persuade them to release the information. See the Federal Open Government Guide (www rcfp.org/fogg/index.php?i=ex1) for further information on any of the specific exemptions cited by the agency in their denial of your original request. The descriptions contained there should suggest arguments you can make to counter the agency's assertions.)

I trust that upon re-consideration, you will reverse the decision denying me access to this material and grant my original request. However, if you deny this appeal, I intend to initiate a lawsuit to compel disclosure. (Don't include this as an idle threat. But if you do intend to fol-low up wtth a lawsuit, say so. Often the agency will more closely consider its positton when it knows it will have to defend it in court soon.)

As I have made this request in the capacity of a journalist (or author, or scholar) and this information is of timely value, I would appreciate your expediting the consideration of my appeal in every way possible. In any case, I will expect to receive your deciston within 20 business days, as required by the statute.

Thank you for your assistance.

Very truly yours,

Your signature

Part Four Review

- Records released under freedom of information require careful scrutiny: Be sure to make notes and ask questions.

- Material may be withheld from release due to exemptions intended to protect sensitive information.

- Confidences of cabinet are generally excluded from the federal law.

- Key institutions including Parliament and the judiciary are not covered.

- Dissatisfied requesters have a right to complain to an ombudsman.

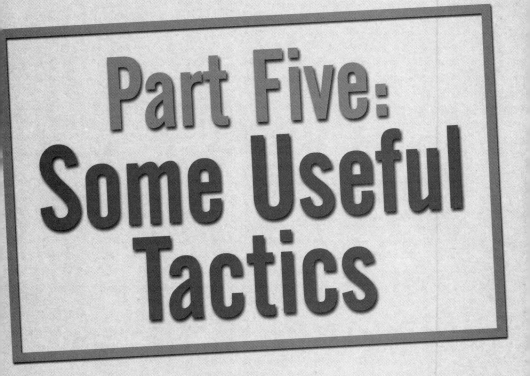

Part Five: Some Useful Tactics

14
Piggybacking

Filing a freedom-of-information request, though a valuable exercise, can be anything but straightforward or a sure thing. This is why it's important to adopt additional tactics that will provide a better chance of success.

Piggybacking, the practice of jumping on to another request, is one of them.

Let's say you're researching the controversy over the proposed Northern Gateway pipeline in Western Canada — a topic that has generated a lot of discussion and media attention. You might want to know more about the planned pipeline route, or what kind of consultations the project's proponent, Enbridge, has been conducting with local residents. Chances are someone else — the environmental group Greenpeace comes to mind — has already requested similar information. If this is the case, then you have the right to jump on, or join, that request by asking that the records be released to you at about the same time, though sometimes they will arrive shortly after the original requester receives them.

This is best done by contacting the relevant agency's coordinator to see if there are requests of interest working their way through the system. The access office won't release the individual's name, which is considered private information, but the duty to assist compels the co-ordinator or analyst to make a check on your behalf.

There is no fee to piggyback on a request. Even if the original requester ends up paying fees in addition to the initial $5 application charge, you don't have to fork out a cent. This is because once the record is released to the first requester, it is considered to be public.

The only downside is that you lack the rights of the original requester, namely the ability to formally complain about any exemptions in the records. However, the time savings and minimal effort may make the trade-off worthwhile.

In the US, federal agencies track requests through *Freedom of Information Act* Logs, which include a brief description of the request, the date it was received, the case status, and — unlike in Canada — usually the name of the requester. While these logs are often posted on agency websites, they can also be requested under the information law.

As in Canada, the listings can be used for piggybacking purposes or, in the case of completed requests, for seeking records already released to others. We will look at previously released records in Chapter 15.

15
Previously Released, Archival, and Overlooked Records

1. Previously Released Records

The most satisfying and worthwhile requests you file will spring from your own initiative: the research you do on a topic of interest, tips you pick up from informed sources, or follow-up ideas that emerge from records released under the information laws. Having said this, sometimes another researcher has already done much of the work for you, and there is no need to file a request of your own. At the very least, the fruits of a completed request can often supplement your original inquiries.

As part of a federal commitment to make data more accessible, the institutions covered by the *Access to Information Act* are required to post summaries[1] of completed requests within 30 calendar days after the end of each month. Links to these summaries are usually found in the Transparency section of an agency's website.

As discussed in the previous chapter, US agencies produce *Freedom of Information Act* logs listing summaries of the requests they have received and processed — a valuable means of quickly finding records released to others that you can now request. These logs are often found on agency websites.

---

1 "Completed Access to Information Requests," Data.gc.ca, accessed September, 2014.
  http://data.gc.ca/eng/completed-access-information-requests

Another noteworthy US initiative,[2] found at foiaonline.regulations.gov, is an omnibus portal that allows users to make requests, track their status, search for requests filed by others, and download copies of processed records. However, at this writing just a handful of federal agencies were participating,

2. Archival Records

Public agencies generally retain records for several years. They also follow policies and schedules that eventually result in those records either being destroyed or sent to the government archives for preservation.

It means Library and Archives Canada[3] is by far the largest record holder in the federal sphere, a valuable repository of information for the requester curious about the historical dimensions of an issue. The institution has an increasingly robust online presence, making available a growing collection of digitized textual records and photographs. The website is also a starting place to search for materials, locate finding aids, or submit questions about holdings. This is the tip of our proverbial iceberg — a sampling of many kilometres of documents, newspapers, photos, films, artwork, maps, and books that constitute a significant portion of Canada's recorded heritage.

Provinces, territories, cities, towns, universities, churches, and others also tend archives that can be treasure troves for the intrepid researcher.

Searching for archival records in the United States follows the same general pattern. The National Archives and Records Administration is the keeper of these extensive holdings. As in Canada, the service has an online presence, and provides even greater access to digital copies of records on subjects from the *Declaration of Independence* to the impeachment of Andrew Johnson. The US archives says that the sheets of paper in its collections, laid end to end, would circle the Earth more than 57 times. Of course, the institution also holds a vast array of films, maps, charts, architectural drawings, posters, and electronic records.

While many of these US and Canadian archival records are open to the public, a considerable number — including documents related to defence and security — remain subject to exemptions under the US freedom-of-information or Canadian access laws.

2 FOIAOnline,'accessed September, 2014. https://foiaonline.regulations.gov/foia/action/public/home
3 Library and Archives Canada, accessed September, 2014. www.lac-bac.gc.ca

In Canada, Library and Archives has an Access to Information division that handles formal requests, but analysts also conduct informal reviews of records for viewing onsite at the institution's Ottawa facilities. The institution's website can answer initial questions about your research and help determine whether an in-person visit would be beneficial.

The US National Archives and Records Administration's website[4] has extensive details on how to file a request.

See Sample 19: Illustration of an archival record released under the federal access law. This 1965 entry from the voluminous RCMP security file on firebrand socialist politician Tommy Douglas contains notes of his conversation with peace activist James Endicott on Parliament Hill. (Source: Library and Archives Canada)

3. A Closer Look at Previously Processed Requests

Open-data policies have forced governments to make information more accessible; in this case, summaries of previously released requests. Each month, institutions release summaries of the requests they have processed.

As you can see from the Aboriginal Affairs and Northern Development Canada April 2014 example in Sample 20, there are four columns in the table: the request number, a summary, the general outcome of the request, and the number of pages. This table and its columns represent a standard format that most agencies follow. Once you've perused the summaries for a particular department of interest, you can simply contact the office using the email link at the bottom of the page.

You can also phone or fax, but it's best to copy and paste the four columns of information contained in the summary into the body of an email, with a brief note explaining that you'd like to make an informal request for the records identified in the summary. Officials in the Access to Information office will use the request number to find the records. Indicate how you would prefer to receive the information; on a CD, or by email as a PDF attachment.

Be sure to include a mailing address along with your phone number, in case the agency has any questions. Politely ask that the analyst acknowledge receipt of your request. Institutions often respond within 30 days or less, but can take longer due to workload

---

4 Freedom of Information Act, National Archives, accessed September, 2014.
   http://www.archives.gov/foia/

RCMP 686L

CONTINUATION C-237
REV. 5-63

RE: ▓▓▓▓ Protests and Demonstrations Re: **Negro**
▓▓▓▓▓▓▓▓▓▓▓▓▓▓▓▓▓▓
Civil Rights ▓▓▓▓▓ ▓ Canada   5-4-65.

PAGE

SECRET

POPE, Wm. Harry ✓ ▓▓▓▓

FRANCIS, Lloyd, M.P.

MARKS, ✓Tony ▓▓▓▓▓

MAYOR, ✓Jim ▓▓▓▓▓ - 200 Laurier Ave., Ottawa

6.   On the 14 Mar 65 Est. D.G. McINTYRE observed a meeting between Tommy DOUGLAS (N.D.P. leader) and James ENDICOTT,
while on parliament hill during the aforementioned demonstration. ENDICOTT, after having congratulated DOUGLAS on his speech
mentioned that he had recently been to Saigon. DOUGLAS asked:
"How are things down there," ENDICOTT "Terrible, terrible, just
terrible". DOUGLAS: "How interesting, Jim, How long will you
be in town?" ENDICOTT: "Monday & Tuesday". DOUGLAS: "Well, how
about having lunch with me either Monday or Tuesday?" ENDICOTT:
"I'll call you on Monday and let you know the situation". DOUG-
LAS: "Fine Jim, I'll leave both Monday and Tuesday lunch hours
open for you. Now be sure and call."

7.   ENDICOTT was next observed approached by Art PAPE
who shook hands with him. PAPE took ENDICOTT by the arm and
introduced him to Diane BURROWS ▓▓▓▓▓▓ (Res.:
Belleville, Ont.). They spoke briefly and then ENDICOTT left
the hill in company of an U/M who he parted with at the Chat-
eau Laurier Hotel, Ottawa.

8.   It will be noted that during the singing of "We shall
Overcome" during the period the speeches were being made to the
demonstrators, ENDICOTT had linked hands with DOUGLAS and both
swayed back and forth together singing this song for about 2
minutes.

9.   During the course of the demonstration, ▓▓▓▓▓▓▓▓
▓▓▓▓▓▓ the following
material which was being passed out by SNCC members: "SNCC News
Briefs"; "Citizen's march for Civil Rights"; and also a copy of
"Freedom Songs". (A copy of each is attached hereto as attachments #'s 1, #2 & #3, -(p1) & (P.2).

SAMPLE 20
COMPLETED REQUESTS

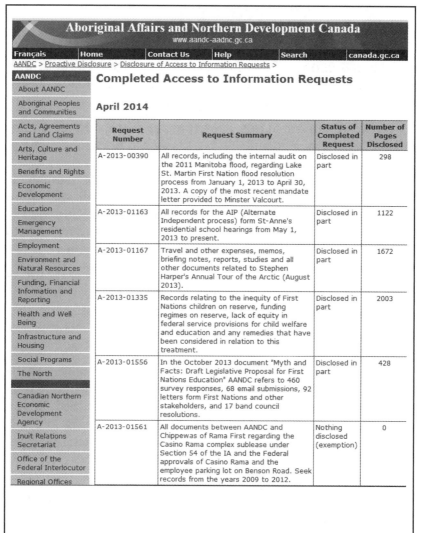

Aboriginal Affairs and Northern Development Canada
www.aandc-aadnc.gc.ca

| Français | Home | Contact Us | Help | Search | canada.gc.ca |

AANDC > Proactive Disclosure > Disclosure of Access to Information Requests >

AANDC
About AANDC

Aboriginal Peoples and Communities

Acts, Agreements and Land Claims

Arts, Culture and Heritage

Benefits and Rights

Economic Development

Education

Emergency Management

Employment

Environment and Natural Resources

Funding, Financial Information and Reporting

Health and Well Being

Infrastructure and Housing

Social Programs

The North

Canadian Northern Economic Development Agency

Inuit Relations Secretariat

Office of the Federal Interlocutor

Regional Offices

Completed Access to Information Requests

April 2014

Request Number	Request Summary	Status of Completed Request	Number of Pages Disclosed
A-2013-00390	All records, including the internal audit on the 2011 Manitoba flood, regarding Lake St. Martin First Nation flood resolution process from January 1, 2013 to April 30, 2013. A copy of the most recent mandate letter provided to Minster Valcourt.	Disclosed in part	298
A-2013-01163	All records for the AIP (Alternate Independent process) form St-Anne's residential school hearings from May 1, 2013 to present.	Disclosed in part	1122
A-2013-01167	Travel and other expenses, memos, briefing notes, reports, studies and all other documents related to Stephen Harper's Annual Tour of the Arctic (August 2013).	Disclosed in part	1672
A-2013-01335	Records relating to the inequity of First Nations children on reserve, funding regimes on reserve, lack of equity in federal service provisions for child welfare and education and any remedies that have been considered in relation to this treatment.	Disclosed in part	2003
A-2013-01556	In the October 2013 document "Myth and Facts: Draft Legislative Proposal for First Nations Education" AANDC refers to 460 survey responses, 68 email submissions, 92 letters form First Nations and other stakeholders, and 17 band council resolutions.	Disclosed in part	428
A-2013-01561	All documents between AANDC and Chippewas of Rama First regarding the Casino Rama complex sublease under Section 54 of the IA and the Federal approvals of Casino Rama and the employee parking lot on Benson Road. Seek records from the years 2009 to 2012.	Nothing disclosed (exemption)	0

pressures and the popularity of this method of obtaining records. Some agencies, particularly ones that have dealt with you in the past, may be willing to expedite the processing of this informal request.

There is no fee, given that the original requester has already paid for the information, which is now a public record. As with piggybacking, the only drawback is that, as an informal requester, you have no right to complain.

If you are interested in a subject matter that spans many institutions, use the search engine[5] that allows you to retrieve summaries simultaneously from many agencies. Or you can download a file[6] in the database or CSV format that contains all the summaries. Knowing how to use Excel spreadsheet software will allow you to open the file and conduct more precise searches. Once you've identified records of interest, you may end up making requests to different access offices that have produced the summaries.

Making an informal request for previously released records is much like filing a formal application, in that service varies widely across the federal government, and some agencies post summaries promptly and provide records within days while others can take several weeks.

The information commissioner's office, which is subject to the law, will email previously released records. At least one federal agency — the CBC — posts a selection of actual released files on its site, eliminating the need to request them. The British Columbia government and many US agencies also make documents available online — efforts that one hopes become part of a trend.

Agencies in both Canada and the United States maintain physical reading rooms where you can browse previously released records. However, US agencies are far ahead in creating electronic reading rooms that feature some of the most popular and commonly requested records released under the American law.

The Federal Bureau of Investigation has uploaded hundreds of fascinating record sets. If you are interested in FBI case files on the Lindbergh baby kidnapping, famous spy capers, notorious gangster Al Capone, or the glamorous Marilyn Monroe, you can

---

5 "Completed Access to Information Requests Search," Data.gc.ca, accessed September, 2014.
  http://data.gc.ca/eng/search/ati?
6 "Access to Information Requests Search," Data.gc.ca, accessed September, 2014.
  http://data.gc.ca/eng/search/ati?

view the documents in The Vault,[7] a special section of the bureau's website. To learn more about FBI records, visit http://www.fbi.gov/foia/a-guide-to-conducting-research-in-fbi-records.

4. Overlooked Records

The majority of records processed under access laws are textual documents, from emails and letters to briefing notes and reports. But in the multimedia era, governments hold more and more records in different formats, as well as some text-based documents you may not have thought about.

They include:

- Photographs. Agencies use photos to enliven their websites or for inclusion in official publications. It's worth seeking the ones that never make it to print.

- Videos. Almost any handheld device can shoot video these days, making such records more common. Videos are often used to train employees, offering insight into departmental roles and duties.

- Audio recordings. Records from crash investigations frequently include audio of conversations between controllers and airline pilots or ship captains. These can vividly convey the circumstances of an accident.

- Newsletters. Many agencies have more employees than a small town and use internal publications — much like a local newspaper — to keep them informed. These are old-fashioned, print-style newsletters or online publications that provide a glimpse into an organization.

- Electronic databases. Departments collect and analyze all manner of statistics, often using standard organizational tools such as Excel spreadsheets or proprietary software to keep track of the numbers. Such databases can be a valuable source of information, one we will explore in the next chapter.

Some of these records may be captured by the wording of your request; remember, the term "records" can include just about anything, but the ones noted above may be overlooked even by the access analyst unless you specifically request them. Info Source,

---

7   "FBI Records: The Vault," Federal Bureau of Investigation (FBI), fbi.gov, accessed September, 2014. http://vault.fbi.gov

which contains detailed listings of departmental holdings, can provide clues as to what kind of records exist, including the format.

In Sample 21, you can see a video still of Polish immigrant Robert Dziekanski, shown at the Vancouver airport in the Canada Border Services Agency closed-circuit camera footage. Dziekanski would die a short time later after being hit with an RCMP Taser stungun.

At the Canadian Security Intelligence Service, even the employee newsletters are classified (see Sample 22). Some material in an article about CSIS memorabilia sales has been exempted from release under the *Access to Information Act*.

SAMPLE 21
ILLUSTRATION OF VIDEO OBTAINED UNDER THE FEDERAL ACCESS LAW

ILLUSTRATION OF A NEWSLETTER OBTAINED UNDER THE FEDERAL ACCESS LAW

Intercom CSIS Corporate Newsletter

Protected
October 2010

CSIS Memorabilia - A Tangible Sense of Belonging

By

Over the years, memorabilia at the Service has evolved a great deal. Long before the CSIS crest was featured on the CSIS Memorabilia collection, the beaver was the unofficial emblem.

In 1986, the industrious Canadian beaver was at the height of fashion, featured on everything from trendy "Roots" Canada sweatshirts to Ottawa's "Beaver Tail" pastry franchises. Tourists flocking to Canada often returned home with a memento of Canada's iconic animal, even if it was simply a Canadian nickel in their pocket. For   drawing a beaver as the unofficial mascot of his graduating IO class must have seemed a natural fit. And it wasn't long before others agreed. Internal Security quickly adopted   beaver for their security awareness posters, which focused on themes of discretion and the need-to-know principle. It was that same notion of discretion that led the beaver to become the unofficial emblem of CSIS Memorabilia items; only those who had the "need-to-know" (ie. employees and partners) could associate the beaver logo with the Service.

However, as the Service grew out of its infancy and strengthened its ties with the international intelligence community, it became increasingly evident that, like all fashion, the beaver's time as the brand identity of CSIS had come to an end. In 2004, former Director Ward Elcock phased out the beaver as the unofficial emblem of CSIS Memorabilia. It was the end of an era and the event was marked by the formal burial of the stuffed toy beaver that resided at NHQ. From this point on, CSIS Memorabilia featured the official CSIS crest.

For the Self-Serve Store's visitors and customers, the CSIS crest has been a suitable replacement. "Our most popular product would have to be our pins. We sell over one hundred a month!" says   the project leader. A variety of clients, from employees to domestic and foreign officials, find their way to the shop tucked away in the lower level of NHQ. "When taking visitors down to the store, they're like kids in a candy shop, because CSIS Memorabilia is something special that they can't find anywhere else," explains

In 2010, the volunteer team responsible for the CSIS Memorabilia project decided to modernize and expand its merchandise line to include items such as hoodies, golf polos and watches. From time to time, the team also receives recommendations for new articles. "To name a few, we've received suggestions for teddy bears, ties, pyjama pants and watches," says. As a matter of fact, it was after receiving a suggestion from an employee that a watch was introduced to the collection.

Items are sold at the initial cost price, and all of the funds received from sold merchandise are put towards purchasing new items. The team strives to balance quality and affordability in their selection and tracks sales to ensure that they are supplying articles that are in demand. "Seeing as the products represent the Service, we recognize the importance of providing memorabilia of superior quality,"

Which leads one to the reoccurring question: where can an employee wear CSIS apparel? Although the clothing does not display the Service's acronym, it does feature the emblem. Some may argue that the majority of Canadian citizens do not recognize our crest, but given the internet and the Service's increasing media presence, the public is gaining awareness of its symbolism. Internal Security would like to remind employees that while the Service does allow memorabilia, what guides its use can be found in   The policy essentially states that employees should exercise discretion in disclosing employment outside the work environment. Furthermore, employees working in   must be particularly vigilant in concealing their employer or any association with CSIS.

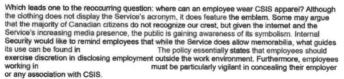

16
Data

Many federal institutions rely on databases to store information that track activities. There are confidential ones for internal personnel issues as well as more public data sets to record events such as train derailments, oil pipeline leaks, the RCMP's use of Taser stun guns, and medical device recalls.

The data is stored in tables with rows and columns. Some tables are relatively small, containing dozens of columns and rows like the database from Health Canada in Table 4 that chronicles the problems caused by faulty medical devices. Other data sets are larger, with rows numbering in the thousands or millions, and columns in the dozens.

In this case, the date of the event is important, as is the "Incident Desc" column that describes what happened. Some personal information has been exempted from the "User Institute" column, but much useful information has been disclosed.

When requesting information contained in tables like Table 4 above, be sure to ask for it in "database format" such as Excel spreadsheets, or text files that can be imported into Excel. Insist that you do not want the tables in PDF format, a scan that freezes the data on the page and doesn't allow for the kinds of sorting and filtering that could uncover crucial trends in the public interest.

Requesting a database can be tricky unless, through diligent research, you have discovered its name and information about the contents. In most instances, you may generally know that the institution uses a database to track a particular activity (e.g., workplace safety violations, inspections of veterans' hospitals), but may lack details about the specific information it holds. In such a case, it's worth including a paragraph in your request seeking a conversation with the keeper of the data — a chat you can use as a starting point to negotiate for parts of the data set that are not subject to the kinds of exemptions we've already discussed. This can be a more involved process, but it is usually worth the effort.

For instance, obtaining a database of medical device recalls for a five-year period, filtering it by the type of device, and then grouping and counting the recalls by year, may show that the device you're looking into has become a problem worth writing about.

Though institutions tend to comply with requests for data in electronic formats such as Excel, or a text file, you may still encounter resistance. Some federal departments insist on releasing tables in static PDF format, defeating the purpose of the database software. (Ironically, this continues to happen at the federal level despite a highly touted effort by the government to release more data sets proactively through a central portal.[1]) If the institution refuses to budge, complain to the information commissioner, as the Access to Information Act says applicants are entitled to "timely access to the record in the format requested."

Despite the popularity of Excel, some government data is stored using proprietary software, meaning it would be difficult to do much with the data even if it were released in electronic format. If release of data in paper form is the only option, you can still manually enter the information into a database you create from scratch.

Generally speaking, US institutions such as the Food and Drug Administration,[2] the National Transportation Safety Board,[3] and the US Department of Labour[4] post data sets that, in Canada, would only be available through access to information. Still, freedom-of-information laws are often needed to obtain US data at the federal or state levels.

---

1 Data.gc.ca, Government of Canada, accessed September, 2014. http://data.gc.ca/data/en/dataset
2 "Electronic Reading Room," US Food and Drug Administration, accessed October, 2014. www.fda.gov/RegulatoryInformation/foi/ElectronicReadingRoom/default.htm
3 "Investigations," National Transportation Safety Board, accessed October 2014. www.ntsb.gov/investigations/databases.html
4 "Data Catalog," US Department of Labor, accessed October 2014. http://ogesdw.dol.gov/views/data_catalogs.php

Table 4
DATABASE

	Entry Dt	Incident Desc	Receipt Dt	Priority	User Institute	Close Dt	Source Of Recall	Investigator	Investigator2	Inc Aware Dt	Final Due Dt	Final Rec Dt
	B	C	D	E	F	G	H	I	J	K	L	M
2	09/Mar/11	***NOT REVIEWED BY CO*** IT WAS REPORTED THE LEAD WAS REPLACED DUE TO OVERSING AND INAPPROPRIATE SHOCKS. NO PATIENT COMPLICATIONS HAVE	09/Dec/30	I	s.19(1)	09/Aug/17	C	SHOPEWEL		08/Dec/08	10/Mar/30	
3	09/Mar/04	***NOT REVIEWED BY CO*** DURING A LEAD REVISION, AIMING TO CORRECT T-WAVE OVERSENSING, THE HEALTH CARE PROFESSIONAL NOTED	09/Dec/18	I	s.19(1)	09/Sep/09	C	SHOPEWEL		08/Nov/17	10/Mar/18	
4	09/Mar/02	***NOT REVIEWED BY CO*** THE PATIENT EXPERIENCED LACK OF EFECTIVE, THERAPEUTIC STIMULATION. THE LEAD WERE REPOSITIONED. THE IMPLANTABLE	09/Dec/15	I	s.19(1)	09/Oct/02	C	YZHANG		08/Nov/14	10/Mar/15	
5	09/Sep/30	ON 9/21/09, A CUSTOMER/LAYPERSON REPORTED TO LIFESCAN THE BLOOD GLUCOSE RESULTS OBTAINED BY USING HER ONETOUCH ULTRA2 METER WERE	09/Sep/30	I	19(1)		C	SEGSTROM		09/Sep/21	09/Dec/29	09/Dec/18
6	09/Sep/30	ON SEPTEMBER 21, 2009, THE LAY USER/PATIENT CONTACTED LIFESCAN (LFS) CANADA ALLEGING THAT HER ONETOUCH ULTRA2 METER WAS PROMPTING A	09/Sep/30	I	19(1)		C	SEGSTROM		09/Sep/21	09/Dec/29	09/Dec/15

Part Five Review

- Piggyback on requests that have already been filed to save time and effort.

- Previously released records can also be a valuable resource.

- Use the federal access law to tap into the huge repository of records held by Library and Archives Canada.

- Don't forget overlooked records such as photos, videos, and audio recordings.

- Government agencies hold an array of information that can be released in databases, making it easy to sort and analyze.

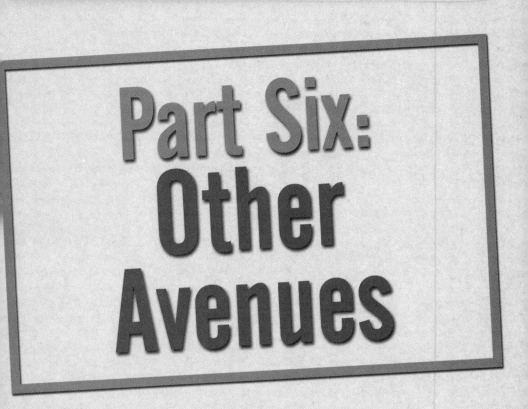

Part Six:
Other
Avenues

17
The Privacy Acts

So far, we've focused on the *Access to Information Act*, but there's another side of federal law governing the flow of information: The *Privacy Act*.[1] This law, which also has provincial and territorial counterparts, limits the federal government's collection, use, and disclosure of personal information.

The government needs a law to safeguard privacy because it holds some kind of personal information about virtually everyone in Canada. Much of it is rather routine in nature, since every year individuals hand over private data to institutions including the Canada Revenue Agency (income tax); the Canada Border Services Agency (the declaration of goods at ports of entry); Citizenship and Immigration Canada (visa application); and Veterans Affairs (files on former military personnel), to name just a handful.

The law gives you the right to request this information and to ask that corrections be made should any errors turn up in the files.

In less common circumstances, agencies such as the RCMP or the Canadian Security Intelligence Service may gather information about you as part of an investigation. While you also have a right to request this information, it may be exempt from release due to the sensitivity and ongoing nature of the probes.

---

1 *Privacy Act*, Government of Canada, accessed September, 2014.
   http://laws-lois.justice.gc.ca/eng/acts/P-21/

People have a reasonable expectation[2] that the information about them held by government agencies is confidential, and the Office of the Privacy Commissioner is the watchdog that ensures material intended to be protected remains under wraps.

Canadian veterans made headlines after obtaining records that revealed mishandling of their personal details. The most celebrated case was that of Sean Bruyea, who sued[3] the government after learning Veterans Affairs had "unlawfully released (personal records) to several employees of Veterans Affairs who were not involved in the delivery of services to him, but who were employed in the implementation of government policy regarding Veterans."

Testifying before the standing committee on Veterans Affairs on April 15, 2010, Bruyea explained how he used the *Privacy Act* to obtain 13,000 pages of personal information. "What emerges from this information is a clearly documented and disturbing picture of public servants seeking reprisals against me specifically for my advocacy work," he explained at the time to shocked MPs on the committee.

Federal agencies handle as many requests for personal records as they do applications for other kinds of government information. In 2012–2013, the latest year for which statistics are available,[4] offices received 55,355 requests, a 9.6 percent increase over the previous fiscal year.

The co-ordinators who handle Access to Information requests also answer privacy requests, which is why their offices are known as ATIP units — for Access to Information and Privacy — denoting the dual nature of their responsibilities.

Making a *Privacy Act* request is much like making an *Access to Information* request, though there is a separate forms[5] and no application fee. If writing a letter, be clear that you're requesting information under the privacy law. As with Access to Information, a range of exemptions apply to records, and agencies may take extensions. However, you have the right to complain to the Office

---

2 "Report on the *Privacy Act*," Office of the Privacy Commissioner of Canada, accessed September, 2014. https://www.documentcloud.org/documents/1212691-report-on-the-privacy-act-2012-2013. html#document/p9/a165156
3 Sean Bruyea Statement of Claim, SeanBruyea.com, accessed September, 2014. http://www.seanbruyea.com/wp-content/uploads/BruyeaClaim.pdf
4 "Requests under the *Privacy Act*: 2012–13," Infosource.gc.ca, accessed September, 2014. http://www.infosource.gc.ca/bulletin/2013/b/bulletin36b03-eng.asp#s7
5 "Personal Information Request Form," Treasury Board of Canada Secretariat, accessed October, 2014. http://www.tbs-sct.gc.ca/tbsf-fsct/350-58-eng.asp

of the Privacy Commissioner[6] about the handling or outcome of your request.

The process for filing a *Privacy Act* request in the United States is much the same. You can either fill out a form or write a letter to the institution in question, asking for information about yourself, or another individual, as long as that person consents.

For instance, if you were making a privacy request to the US Department of Justice[7], you would write a letter, or fill out a form.[8] Be sure to provide enough detail that would allow staff to identify the relevant records.

If you are seeking records about yourself, you'll be required to verify your identity in order to ensure that they are not improperly disclosed to someone else.

The department, like most others in the US, accepts the requests electronically.

There is no fee. Departments have 20 working days to respond, though that length of time can vary depending on circumstances such as workload and the complexity of the request.

Upon receipt of your request, the department will send an acknowledgement letter with a tracking number. We suggest the same kind of attention to follow-up discussed in earlier chapters to ensure maximum success.

If the request takes longer, you'll be notified of an extension. As in Canada, the outcome of a *Privacy Act* request may be appealed.

---

6 Office of the Privacy Commissioner of Canada, accessed September, 2014. https://www.priv.gc.ca
7 "FOIA Frequently Asked Questions," US Department of Justice, accessed October, 2014.
    www.justice.gov/usao/resources/foiarequests/foia_faq.html
8 "Certification of Identity", US Department of Justice, accessed October, 2014.
    www.justice.gov/sites/default/files/oip/legacy/2014/07/23/cert_ind.pdf

Table 5
PRIVACY REQUESTS IN 2012-2013

A Requests Under the *Privacy Act*	B Number of Requests
Received during 2012–13 reporting period	55,355
Outstanding from 2011–12 reporting period	9,867
Total	**65,222**
Closed during 2012–13 reporting period	56,059
Carried over to 2013–14 reporting period	9,163

Source: Info Source Bulletin Number 36B — Statistical Reporting

18
Reform

Canada's *Access to Information Act* — once a leading-edge tool — has become rather old-fashioned in many eyes since taking force in 1983. It has barely changed over the last three decades while other countries have leapfrogged ahead.

As a result, Canada's act sits in 56th spot on a list of freedom-of-information laws from 98 countries analyzed by the Halifax-based Centre for Law and Democracy[1] and Access Info Europe, just behind Colombia and Mongolia.

"Canada's lax timelines, imposition of access fees, lack of a proper public interest override, and blanket exemptions for certain political offices all contravene international standards for the right of access," says an accompanying report.[2]

"Canada's antiquated approach to access to information is also the result of a lack of political will to improve the situation."

A 2012 assessment by the centre placed the federal law in a tie for last place, with Alberta and New Brunswick, among Canadian access regimes.

"Every jurisdiction in Canada fared poorly from an international perspective," said the report.

"The three biggest problems, all of which recur in every Canadian law, are limits on scope in terms of public authorities (covered

1 Centre for Law and Democracy, accessed September, 2014. www.law-democracy.org/live
2 "Canadian RTI Rating," Centre for Law and Democracy, accessed September, 2014.
   www.law-democracy.org/live/global-rti-rating/canadian-rti-rating

by the laws), procedural weaknesses, and overly broad regimes of exceptions."

There have been numerous calls from pro-democracy groups and the federal information commissioner's office over the years to modernize the national law for the 21st century.

Prospects for change looked bright in early 2006 when Stephen Harper's Conservatives took office following promises[3] to introduce sweeping reforms to the law that would make a greater range of information more readily accessible and give the information commissioner more power.

Harper has so far broken those promises, leaving the law almost untouched. His unfulfilled pledges would do the following:

- Give the information commissioner the power to order the release of information.

- Subject the exclusion of cabinet confidences to review by the commissioner.

- Provide a general public interest override for all exemptions so that the public interest is put before government secrecy.

- Ensure all exemptions from the disclosure of government information are justified only on the basis of the harm or injury that would result from disclosure, not blanket exemption rules.

- Ensure the disclosure requirements of the Act cannot be circumvented by secrecy provisions in other federal laws, while respecting the confidentiality of national security and the privacy of personal information.

As we have noted, the government did expand the scope of the Act to include Crown corporations such as Canada Post, the CBC, and Via Rail. However, key entities, including the House of Commons and Senate, remain excused from the law.

Instead of overhauling the Act, the federal government has focused on making data sets easier to locate and download through the creation of a central portal. As part of its commitment to the Open Government Partnership[4] — a US-led movement to increase

---

3 "Conservative Party Federal Election Platform 2006," Poltext.org, accessed September, 2014.
   www.poltext.org/sites/poltext.org/files/plateformes/can2006pc_plt_en._14112008_165519.pdf
4 Open Government Partnership, accessed September, 2014. www.opengovpartnership.org

global openness — Canada has also promised to create a virtual library of government documents, improve federal record-keeping, make more archival material accessible, and introduce online request capability.

Democracy Watch,[5] an Ottawa-based lobby group, says the plan will only make some government information more easily available in electronic format — not truly improve openness or accountability.

The federal government is developing a second round of commitments for the Open Government Partnership, to be finalized in 2015.

As of this writing, Information Commissioner[6] Suzanne Legault plans to release her own report with recommendations on reforming the *Access to Information Act*, drawing on consultations with interested parties and her own experiences with the law.

Legault's review[7] began two years ago on the tenth anniversary of Right to Know Day, which has roots in an international gathering of access-to-information advocates in Bulgaria in 2002.

"We really wanted to look at a broad range of models, and look at the best solutions that are out there," Legault said at the time. "And this exercise will allow us to have that kind of review."

In the United States, there are also calls for reform. And they're getting louder.

There were great expectations on January 21, 2009, when US President Barack Obama marked his first day in office by issuing two memoranda for the Heads of Executive Departments and Agencies. One memo focused on the administration of the *Freedom of Information Act*[8]; the second centred on Transparency and Open Government[9].

While the words were encouraging, with references to "creating unprecedented openness" and the requirement for agencies to adopt the "presumption of disclosure," there are still many calls for reform — calls that echo those in Canada.

5 Democracy Watch, accessed September, 2014. http://democracywatch.ca
6 Office of the Information Commissioner of Canada, accessed September, 2014. www.oic-ci.gc.ca
7 "Canadas Information Commissioner Opens a Dialogue on the *Access to Information Act*," Office of the Information Commissioner of Canada, accessed September, 2014. www.oic-ci.gc.ca/eng/media-room-salle-media_news-releases-communiques-de-presse_2012_7.aspx
8 *"Freedom of Information Act*, memorandum for the Heads of Executive Departments and Agencies," the White House, accessed October, 2014. www.whitehouse.gov/the_press_office/FreedomofInformationAct
9 "Transparency and Open Government," the White House, accessed October, 2014. www.whitehouse.gov/the_press_office/TransparencyandOpenGovernment

Concerns grew when the US Department of Veterans Affairs blocked release of the names of hospitals where 19 veterans died under suspicious circumstances[10].

In a significant bi-partisan response, Democratic Senator Patrick Leahy, chairman of the Senate Judiciary Committee, and Republican John Cornyn[11] put forward a bill demanding reforms. The legislation would turn Obama's suggestion that agencies adopt a presumption of openness into a legal requirement. As well, the bill would reduce the number of exemptions agencies are allowed to use, and invest the Office of Government Information Services with greater powers to fulfill its ombudsman function.

"The *Freedom of Information Act* is one of our nation's most important laws, established to give Americans greater access to their government and to hold government accountable," Leahy said in a news release outlining his concerns.

---

10 "Outrage as V.A. hides names of hospitals where vets died from delays," *The Washington Times,* accessed October, 2014. www.washingtontimes.com/news/2014/mar/31/outrage-v-hides-names-hospitals-where-vets-died-de/?page=all
11 "Congress Moving on FOIA Reform," The National Security Archives, accessed October, 2014. www2.gwu.edu/~nsarchiv/news/20140624/

Conclusion

We have indeed come a long way since the Age of Enlightenment and Sweden's passage of the first access law in 1766. Governments have become more complex and influential in our lives. Our rights to hold them to account have grown, if not proportionally, then to a degree that should give us increasing comfort. However, there is still a lot of work to be done, which is one of the reasons we hope this book will help you get started.

In a wired world where information is available at the click of a mouse or the swipe of a mobile screen, freedom of information may seem quaint, even archaic. The notion of filling out forms, writing cheques, and sending off letters in the mail — only to wait weeks or months for a response — might make you wonder why you even bothered learning about all this in the first place.

Trust us: Like a slow-cooked meal that's worth spending hours in the kitchen, freedom of information is a profitable investment for the serious researcher. As with cooking, you don't have to be an expert to succeed at filing access requests. The main ingredients are a bit of preparation, patience, and stick-to-it-iveness — the refusal to give up after the first, or even the fifth, discouraging episode.

Though Canada's federal access and privacy laws are imperfect and in need of reform, an increasing number of people are using them, and proponents of reform continue to push for change. After trying your hand at making federal requests, you may notice aspects that need improvement. If so, speak up. If you feel the law should be strengthened to allow for the release of more information, or for greater powers that would help the information commissioner better investigate complaints, then contact your member of Parliament[1] to share your views. Pressure for reform must begin from the ground up.

Use the law for your town or city to ask about a neighbourhood concern. Try the provincial or territorial act. File a federal request about that issue you've always wondered about. Try your hand at filing a request in the United States to see how issues of cross-border concern such as meat safety are playing out. These laws belong to you, helping facilitate your legal right to records created on your behalf.

There will be delays, setbacks, and challenges. There will also be days when you open your mailbox to find a manila envelope full of information that will reward your curiosity and perseverance.

---

1 "Members of the House of Commons," Parliament of Canada, accessed September, 2014. www.parl.gc.ca/parlinfo/Lists/Members.aspx?Language=E&SortColumn=PartyName&SortDirection =ASC&Parliament=1924d334-6bd0-4cb3-8793-cee640025ff6&Riding=&Name=&Party=&Province =&Gender=&New=False&Current=False&First=False&Picture=True&Section=False&ElectionDate=

Appendix I:
Tips for Journalists

Freedom of information can be an especially helpful tool for journalists in the age of strict government message control. Here are some tips to help reporters get the most out of the laws:

- Identify the uniquely created records (e.g., inspection reports, incident logs, and meeting minutes) in the agencies you follow. Ask for them on a regular basis.

- Make a rolling list of ideas to keep handy for those spare moments when you can prepare and send a few requests.

- Consider filing a request after a major news event has captured headlines, or as a follow up to one of your own stories.

- Keep the information pipeline full by filing requests at least once a month.

- Once you have received records, carefully review them, identify a potential story, and seek comment from the agency that created them. Asking questions can help clarify the nature of the records as well as provide an essential viewpoint for your story. In fact, the records now in your hands could persuade an agency to comment on an issue it would rather not discuss.

- An agency's media relations division likely will be aware of records being released to you, but don't be surprised if spokespeople ask to see a copy of the records to help them prepare comment.

- Share the records with other potential sources such as opposition politicians, interest groups, and individuals affected by the relevant issue to provide a range of perspectives for your story.

Appendix II:
Sources for Further Reading

Freedominfo.org
   www.freedominfo.org

Right2Info
   www.right2info.org/

Access Info
   www.access-info.org/

All About Information
   http://allaboutinformation.ca/

Anders Chydenius
   www.chydenius.net/eng/articles/artikkeli.
   asp?id=1021&referer=1&pages=1

"The World's First Freedom of Information Act: Anders
Chydenius' Legacy Today"
   www.access-info.org/documents/Access_Docs/Thinking/
   Get_Connected/worlds_first_foia.pdf

Centre for Law and Democracy
www.law-democracy.org/

"Brokering Access: Power, Politics, and Freedom of Information Process in Canada"
www.ubcpress.ca/books/pdf/chapters/2012/
BrokeringAccess.pdf

Digging deeper: A Canadian reporter's research guide, by Robert Cribb, Dean Jobb, David McKie, and Fred Vallance-Jones
www.oupcanada.com/higher_education/companion/comm_
studies/9780195432305.html

Canada

Access to Information Act
http://laws-lois.justice.gc.ca/eng/acts/A-1/

Privacy Act
http://laws-lois.justice.gc.ca/eng/acts/P-21/

Federal Departments and Agencies
http://canada.ca/en/gov/dept/index.html

Info Source (directory of holdings)
www.infosource.gc.ca/index-eng.asp

Open Data Portal
http://data.gc.ca/

Access to Information and Privacy Coordinators
www.tbs-sct.gc.ca/atip-aiprp/apps/coords/index-eng.asp

Personal Information Request Form
http://www.tbs-sct.gc.ca/tbsf-fsct/350-58-eng.asp

Access to Information Request Form
www.tbs-sct.gc.ca/tbsf-fsct/350-57_e.asp

Lodging a Complete Form

www.oic-ci.gc.ca/eng/lc-cj-lodge-complaint-deposer-planite.aspx

Specific Exemptions under the *Access to Information Act* (Treasury Board of Canada Secretariat)

www.tbs-sct.gc.ca/pol/doc-eng.aspx?section=text&id=13784

Office of the Information Commissioner of Canada

www.oic-ci.gc.ca/eng/

Office of the Privacy Commissioner of Canada

www.priv.gc.ca

Provinces and Territories

Alberta

http://foip.alberta.ca/pbdirectory/index.cfm

British Columbia

www.gov.bc.ca/citz/iao/

www.gov.bc.ca/citz/

www.oipc.bc.ca/

www.openinfo.gov.bc.ca/ibc/index.page?

Completed Freedom of Information requests at BCFerries

www.bcferries.com/about/foi/tracker.html

Access in the Academy: Bringing FOI and ATI to Academic Research (BC Freedom of Information and Privacy Association)

https://www.gifttool.com/donations/Donate?ID=1552&AID=2700:

Manitoba

www.gov.mb.ca/chc/fippa/

www.gov.mb.ca/chc/fippa/public_bodies/public_bodies_under_fippa.html

www.gov.mb.ca/chc/fippa/public_bodies/forms.html

Manitoba (Access to information requests — weekly listing)
www.gov.mb.ca/chc/fippa/disclosure.html

New Brunswick

Main

www2.gnb.ca/content/gnb/en/services/services_render-er.200949.html

Law

www.gnb.ca/acts/acts/r-10-3.htm

Newfoundland and Labrador

www.justice.gov.nl.ca/just/info/index.html

Northwest Territories

www.justice.gov.nt.ca/ATIPP/index.shtml

Nova Scotia

Main

www.foipop.ns.ca/

List of departments

http://foipop.ns.ca/PB_Contact

Review

www.foipop.ns.ca/

Right to Know Coalition of Nova Scotia

http://nsrtk.blogspot.ca/

Nunavut

www.gov.nu.ca/access-information-and-protection-privacy-atipp

Ontario

Main and Form

www.ontario.ca/government/how-make-freedom-information-request

Prince Edward Island

www.gov.pe.ca/jps/FOIPPfaqs

Quebec

www.cai.gouv.qc.ca/diffusion-de-linformation/

Quebec access-to-information coordinators

www.cai.gouv.qc.ca/documents/CAI_liste_resp_acces_eng.pdf

Saskatchewan

www.justice.gov.sk.ca/Contacts-by-Institution

Yukon

www.atipp.gov.yk.ca/

United States

Federal

Freedom of Information Act (FOIA)

www.foia.gov

https://foiaonline.regulations.gov/

Federal and State resources

National Freedom of Information Coalition

www.nfoic.org

Reporters Committee for Freedom of the Press

www.rcfp.org/federal-open-government-guide

www.rcfp.org

Request tracking tool

www.ifoia.org/#!/

Accountability

foiaproject.org

The Sunshine in Government Initiative: Promoting Transparency
& Accountability in Government

http://sunshineingovernment.org/

The US National Archives and Records Administration
www.archives.gov

US Food and Drug Administration Electronic Reading Room
www.fda.gov/RegulatoryInformation/foi/ElectronicReading
Room/default.htm

International

Office of the Information of Canada — links to other countries
www.oic-ci.gc.ca/eng/links-liens.aspx

Freedominfo.org — links to other countries
www.freedominfo.org/regions/

Right2info — links to constitutional provisions, laws, and regulations in other countries
http://right2info.org/laws

What Do They Know — Search requests
https://www.whatdotheyknow.com/list/successful

Download Kit

Please enter the URL you see in the box below into your computer web browser to access and download the kit.

www.self-counsel.com/updates/right-to-know/14kit.htm

The kit includes:

- Resources on ways to get information from governments under different acts
- Tips for researchers and journalists
- Further reading resources
- And more!